# THOMAS HARDY
## THE POETRY OF NECESSITY

# THOMAS HARDY
## THE POETRY OF NECESSITY

James Richardson

THE UNIVERSITY OF CHICAGO PRESS
CHICAGO AND LONDON

JAMES RICHARDSON is assistant professor of English at Harvard University and author of *Reservations*, a collection of poems.

THE UNIVERSITY OF CHICAGO PRESS, CHICAGO 60637
THE UNIVERSITY OF CHICAGO PRESS, LTD., LONDON

© 1975, 1977 by The University of Chicago
All rights reserved. Published 1977
Printed in the United States of America
81 80 79 78 77  987654321

**Library of Congress Cataloging in Publication Data**

Richardson, James   1950–
   Thomas Hardy: the poetry of necessity.

   Includes index.
   1. Hardy, Thomas, 1840–1928—Criticism and
interpretation.
PR4754.R5   823'.8   76-8100
ISBN 0-226-71237-0

FOR CECIL Y. LANG

# CONTENTS

# 1
# NECESSITY AND POSSIBILITY

> The lost days of my life until to-day,
>   What were they, could I see them on the street
>   Lie as they fell? Would they be ears of wheat
> Sown once for food but trodden into clay?
> Or golden coins squandered and still to pay?
>   Or drops of blood dabbling the guilty feet?
>   Or such spilt water as in dreams must cheat
> The undying throats of Hell, athirst alway?
>
> I do not see them here; but after death
>   God knows I know the faces I shall see,
> Each one a murdered self, with low last breath.
>   "I am thyself,—what hast thou done to me?"
> "And I—and I—thyself," (lo! each one saith,)
>   "And thou thyself to all eternity!"
>
> "Lost Days," D. G. Rossetti

When the transcendent vanishes, the poet is threatened by mechanical necessity and infinite possibility, assailed by both the arbitrariness and the inevitability of identity. Where the universe leaves off narrowing him, habit begins. Hardy takes full responsibility for his limits even as he struggles to deny them. He retreats to a small world and a modest voice to consider, within the bounds of his care, not only how things are but how they might have been. This interplay of avoidance and investigation, of limitation and multiplicity, of necessity and possibility, accounts for the blend of strength and sentiment which characterizes Hardy's lyrics. Only when life is all we have do its ironies and lost chances become compelling, and yet only then do they verge on meaninglessness.

To say that Hardy was literally a victim of a sudden disappearance of the "transcendent" is to say practically nothing or to place Apocalypse in the mid-nineteenth century. Each generation finds itself expelled from paradise, for paradises are imagined already lost. It is nevertheless true that though Hardy has much in common with his Romantic forebears and though he admired them past idolatry, he was unable and unwilling to repeat their performances. He felt dwarfed by them, but he felt even more strongly the necessity of his diminution, perceiving that their styles, aspirations and modes of thought were, for him, not only impossible but also inappropriate, and perhaps even embarrassing. The traits which Donald Davie sees as Hardy's legacy to modern British poetry, namely ''an apparent meanness of spirit, a painful modesty of intention, extremely limited objectives''[1] are not, for better or for worse, inherent in Romanticism, but they were necessary and comfortable for Hardy, and they follow from his reinterpretation of the purposes and possibilities of poetry. In order to get at the nature, if not the cause, of this change, it would be well to examine Hardy's ambivalence toward his great predecessors.

There is little explicit discussion of this subject, or indeed of any critical subject, in Hardy's writings, for he distrusted and disliked analysis. Instead, he treats poets as landmarks or heroes, recommends them as moral crusaders, and is irresistibly drawn to their gravesites. In ''Shelley's Skylark,'' however, a certain confusion is in evidence:

> Somewhere afield here something lies
> In Earth's oblivious eyeless trust
> That moved a poet to prophecies—
> A pinch of unseen, unguarded dust:
>
> The dust of the lark that Shelley heard,
> And made immortal through times to be;—
> Though it only lived like another bird,
> And knew not its immortality:
>
> Lived its meek life; then, one day, fell—
> A little ball of feather and bone;
> And how it perished, when piped farewell,
> And where it wastes, are alike unknown.
>
> Maybe it rests in the loam I view,
> Maybe it throbs in a myrtle's green,
> Maybe it sleeps in the coming hue
> Of a grape on the slopes of yon inland scene.
>
> Go find it, faeries, go and find
> That tiny pinch of priceless dust,

> And bring a casket silver-lined,
> And framed of gold that gems encrust;

> And we will lay it safe therein,
> And consecrate it to endless time;
> For it inspired a bard to win
> Ecstatic heights in thought and rhyme.
>
> [CP92][2]

The first four stanzas are not at all unusual. For Hardy, home is, overpoweringly, home, and when in these "Poems of Pilgrimage" he journeys to the Continent it is only to find the relics of the saints he has long known—Gibbon, Keats, Joshua, and Shelley. He refuses an invitation to the United States on the grounds that new lands have no familiar ghosts:

> My ardours for emprize nigh lost
> Since Life has bared its bones to me,
> I shrink to seek a modern coast
> Whose riper times have yet to be;
> Where the new regions claim them free
> From that long drip of human tears
> Which peoples old in tragedy
> Have left upon the centuried years.
>
> [CP99]

The last two stanzas of "Shelley's Skylark," however, are uncharacteristically precious and present a real puzzle. They could represent an ironic condemnation of literal-minded nostalgia, but given Hardy's nature this is highly unlikely. Are they a burlesque of Hardy's favorite lyrist or a genuine but absurd and self-conscious imitation of his style? One suspects that Hardy intended neither of these alternatives but committed both. Considering his real distance from Shelley he could hardly do otherwise. In any case, Hardy's attitude is defensive and incoherent, and the lines are embarrassed and embarrassing. They embody his inability to deal with his subject on Shelley's terms and in Shelley's high style. Shelley's mode is invocation, but Hardy's is commemoration. His muse is not the lark ascending but the bird of dust.

Hardy's persistent, implied dialogue with Wordsworth is perhaps more revealing. Many of his poems are, so to speak, bounced off

3

the older poet's vision of a beneficent Nature. "Nature's Questioning" comes immediately to mind:

> When I look forth at dawning, pool,
>   Field, flock, and lonely tree,
>   All seem to gaze at me
> Like chastened children sitting silent in a school;
>   Their faces dulled, constrained, and worn,
>     As though the master's ways
>     Through the long teaching days
> Had cowed them till their early zest was overborne.
>
> [CP58]

The use of "chastened" to explain Nature's reluctance to yield up its sympathy is typical, and indeed both chastening and schooling are prominent in a similar context in *Two on a Tower*:

> he was worshiping the sun. Among the various intensities of that worship which have prevailed since the first intelligent being saw the luminary decline westward, as the young man now beheld it doing, his was not the weakest. He was engaged in what may be called a very chastened or schooled form of that first and most natural of adorations.[3]

Finally, a related word, "chidden," expresses the distance of Nature in "Neutral Tones":

> We stood by a pond that winter day,
> And the sun was white, as though chidden of God,
> And a few leaves lay on the starving sod;
> —They had fallen from an ash, and were gray.
>
> [CP9]

The image of Nature (or of man's enthusiasm for Nature, which becomes the same thing) common to these three passages is certainly non-Wordsworthian, but it is just as certainly not Darwinian. Nature is depicted not as a horror show "red in tooth and claw" from which the poet recoils in disgust, but rather as "chastened," as found out and overpowered by the mind. If the consequence of this intellectual manhandling of the the landscape is dull blankness, a kind of solipsistic revulsion, it is because Hardy has involved himself in what is, for him, an inherently meaningless game. He deliberately comes to Nature with expectations which are

4

not his own, which are, in fact, those he perceives as Wordsworth's, and it is therefore not surprising that what he discovers is nothingness. When Hardy is more nearly himself, his relationship to Nature is more nearly nonmanipulative:

> Let me enjoy the earth no less
> Because the all-enacting Might
> That fashioned forth its loveliness
> Had other aims than my delight.
> [CP222]

Romantic poetry, according to Harold Bloom (and to Hardy) insists on "the power of mind over outward sense":

Romantic nature poetry, despite a long critical history of misrepresentation, was an antinature poetry, even in Wordsworth who sought a reciprocity or even a dialogue with nature, but found it only in flashes.... Bradley stressed the strong side of Wordsworth's imagination, its Miltonic sublimity, which Arnold evidently never noticed, but which accounts for everything that is major in *The Prelude* and in the central crisis lyrics associated with it. Though Wordsworth came as a healer, and Shelley attacked him, in *Mont Blanc,* for attempting to reconcile man with nature, there is no such reconciliation in Wordsworth's poetry, and the healing function is performed only when the poetry shows the power of mind over outward sense. The strength of renovation in Wordsworth resides only in the spirit's splendor, in what he beautifully calls "possible sublimity" or "something ever more about to be," the potential of an imagination too fierce to be contained by nature.[4]

The manipulated or repressed landscape is a constant, and normally effective, feature of Hardy's poetry, but as we shall see in later chapters, what is an end for Wordsworth is a beginning for Hardy, who characteristically rebounds from Nature's rejection of his mind into a discovery which is ultimately more satisfying for him, the discovery of the heroic self-sufficiency of both the mind and the landscape. Hardy says in *The Life of Thomas Hardy*, which was meant to pass as the work of his second wife, "Nature is played out as a Beauty, but not as a Mystery" (L185),[5] and mystery, for

Hardy, does not bear looking into. He treats Nature not as a message but as an independent and entirely inexplicable fellow being whose charm is in its very inaccessibility and irrelevance. It is when he stands determinedly "In Front of the Landscape" as a sightseer bent on extracting something from the scene that he works too hard:

> Plunging and labouring on in a tide of visions,
>   Dolorous and dear,
> Forward I pushed my way as amid waste waters
>   Stretching around,
> Through whose eddies there glimmered the customed
>                                         landscape
> Yonder and near . . . ,
>
>                                    [CP285]

Though it is customary to make much of Wordsworth's use of natural detail, Hardy, when he is not trying to prove a point, is an equally exact and far more frequent observer:

> If it be in the dusk when, like an eyelid's soundless blink,
>   The dewfall-hawk comes crossing the shades to alight
> Upon the wind-warped upland thorn, a gazer may think,
>   "To him this must have been a familiar sight."
>
> If I pass during some nocturnal blackness, mothy and warm,
>   When the hedgehog travels furtively over the lawn,
> One may say, "He strove that such innocent creatures
>                                 should come to no harm,
> But he could do little for them; and now he is gone."
>
>                                    [CP521]

This is certainly as beautiful and respectful a treatment of Nature as anything in Wordsworth. It contains no trace of disillusionment because Hardy is true to himself in leaving Nature alone—his best poems come *with* landscapes, but they are not *about* them. Seen in this light, "Nature's Questioning" is as much an act of criticism as a poem, and it criticizes not so much Nature as what Hardy perceives as the Romantic mind.

Whatever is built upon it by the temperaments of individual poets, the foundation of Romantic nature poetry is a sense of the separateness of objects, a precipitous imbalance in perception, an uncertainty of meaning perhaps similar to that which occurs when we repeat a familiar word over and over until it becomes strange, until it becomes simultaneously a nearly physical entity and a meaningless sound. At one extreme, objects fade and refuse to come into focus, as in

> those obstinate questionings
> Of sense and outward things,
> Fallings from us, vanishings;
> Blank misgivings of a Creature
> Moving about in worlds not realized. . . .

At the other, they assert an ominous singularity, a sheer and disturbing physicality:

> —But there's a Tree, of many, one,
> A single Field which I have looked upon,
> Both of them speak of something that is gone:
>   The Pansy at my feet
>   Doth the same tale repeat:
> Whither is fled the visionary gleam?
> Where is it now, the glory and the dream?

The words, of course, are Wordsworth's, and they represent only one version of the crisis. Blake concentrates more obviously on the internal aspects of the problem and sees the soul as out of touch not only with its objects but also with itself. In *The Book of Thel*, both the objects and Thel herself, who is cut off from experience, fade:

> The daughters of Mne. Seraphim led round their sunny flocks,
> All but the youngest. she in paleness sought the secret air.
> To fade away like morning beauty from her mortal day:
> Down by the river of Adona her soft voice is heard:
> And thus her gentle lamentation falls like morning dew.
>
> O life of this our spring! why fades the lotus of the water?
> Why fade these children of the spring? born but to smile & fall.
> Ah! Thel is like a watry bow, and like a parting cloud,
> Like a reflection in a glass. Like shadows in the water.
> Like dreams of infants. like a smile upon an infant's face,
> Like the doves voice, like transient day, like music in the air . . .

The failure is Thel's, and in the course of the poem it is interpreted in terms of sexual and imaginative timidity. At the other end of the spectrum, objects which assert an alien singularity, which will neither speak nor hear, are associated with iron, which is for Blake the limit of both touch and imagination. "To Winter" furnishes a good example:

> O Winter! bar thine adamantine doors:
> The north is thine; there hast thou built thy dark
> Deep-founded habitation. Shake not thy roofs,
> Nor bend thy pillars with thine iron car.
>
> He hears me not, but o'er the yawning deep
> Rides heavy; his storms are unchain'd; sheathed
> In ribbed steel, I dare not lift mine eyes;
> For he hath reared his sceptre o'er the world.

The "Preludium" to *America a Prophecy* combines all these elements—shadowiness (fading), iron, dumbness, repressed desire—and points the way to Blake's solution (or dissolution) of the problem:

> The shadowy daughter of Urthona stood before red Orc.
> When fourteen suns had faintly journey'd o'er his dark abode;
> His food she brought in iron baskets, his drink in cups of iron;
> Crown'd with a helmet & dark hair the nameless female stood;
> A quiver with its burning stores, a bow like that of night,
> When pestilence is shot from heaven; no other arms she need:
> Invulnerable tho' naked, save where clouds roll round her loins,
> Their awful folds in the dark air; silent she stood as night;
> For never from her iron tongue could voice or sound arise;
> But dumb till that dread day when Orc assay'd his fierce embrace.

In these short poems, as well as in his epics, Blake fights shadow and steel with fire, and his invocation of these distant and unresponsive parts of mind and Nature never escapes its connection with the metaphor of tactility, of sexuality. Shadow and steel are aspects of the same alienation, and Blake repeatedly calls down Apocalypse to abolish them in what is simultaneously an imaginative reintegration and an ecstatic sexual union.

Blake's furor tends to isolate him, to regenerate the divisions it is designed to heal. Nothing could be further from Hardy's considered quietism. The later poet "resolves" the Romantic paradox largely by refusing to admit its existence, or at least by denying the possibility of escape.

We are accustomed to see in Keats the most sensuous Romantic, one whose characteristic apprehension of things is through passionate, but seldom frenetic, naming. His approach to objects is gentle but nevertheless Romantic—he inhabits them. Langbaum jumps from this aspect of Keats to his definition of the "poetry of experience" as the "observer's imaginative penetration of the object to arrive at a meaning which is in the end the informed object—the bird, the mountain, the landscape with the observer inside it. . . . For the observer does not so much learn as become something. Each discovery of the external world is a discovery of himself, of his identity with and difference from the external world."[6]

This will do for Keats, but not, or not without qualification, for Hardy. Langbaum is thinking of the "Ode to a Nightingale," and Hardy's "The Darkling Thrush" provides an instructive contrast. While Keats at least attempts some kind of imaginative penetration, Hardy is almost willfully reluctant to approach his eminently bedraggled thrush:

> I leant upon a coppice gate
>   When Frost was spectre-gray,
> And Winter's dregs made desolate
>   The weakening eye of day.
> The tangled bine-stems scored the sky
>   Like strings of broken lyres,
> And all mankind that haunted nigh
>   Had sought their household fires.
>
> The land's sharp features seemed to be
>   The Century's corpse outleant,
> His crypt the cloudy canopy,
>   The wind his death-lament.
> The ancient pulse of germ and birth
>   Was shrunken hard and dry,
> And every spirit upon earth
>   Seemed fervourless as I.
>
> At once a voice arose among
>   The bleak twigs overhead
> In a full-hearted evensong
>   Of joy illimited;
> An aged thrush, frail, gaunt and small,

In blast beruffled plume,
Had chosen thus to fling his soul
Upon the growing gloom.

So little cause for carolings
  Of such ecstatic sound
Was written on terrestrial things
  Afar or nigh around,
That I could think there trembled through
  His happy good-night air
Some blessed Hope, whereof he knew
  And I was unaware.

[CP137]

This is one of Hardy's most famous poems, and it deserves to be, but it must be said that it is not entirely straightforward, in that Hardy is very consciously writing against, bouncing off, the Romantics. The intellectual manhandling of the landscape in "the land's sharp features seemed to be / The Century's corpse outleant" is one of those slightly gratuitous ironies noted above—though Hardy objected to being called a gloom-monger, he often encouraged his critics by playing the role. "Fervourless" is also a kind of intentional falsification, for if Hardy is almost always melancholy, and sometime mawkishly sentimental, he is seldom, even in his gloomiest poems (and certainly not in this one), "fervourless." These slightly forced notes in Hardy are usually a sign that he is preparing to prove a point, and it would not be irresponsible to guess that in this case the point concerns Keats's "Ode" and its visionary uses of Nature. The last two stanzas, in their stubborn refusal to follow Keats's flight, also embody a kind of irony, but this irony is the result not of contrivance but of a profound difference in temperament, and it is, in fact, the poem's main source of strength.

David Perkins, after noting "verbal echoes suggesting that the 'Ode to a Nightingale,' in particular, may have been stirring in Hardy's consciousness (the '*Darkling* Thrush' recalling '*Darkling* I listen,' '*spectre*-gray' echoing 'youth grows . . . *spectre* thin,' '*full-hearted* evensong' paralleling '*full-throated* ease;' the thrush choosing to '*fling his soul*' with 'so little cause for . . . such *ecstatic sound,'* while the nightingale in Keats' 'Ode' is *'pouring forth thy soul* abroad/In such an *ecstasy')"* concludes that "in Hardy's poem . . . there is no hope of closing the gap between speaker and bird."[7] This is probably true for Keats as well as Hardy—what differentiates "The Darkling Thrush" from the "Ode" is that Hardy does not *attempt* to close the gap, and that the poem achieves its peculiar success through its refusal of what for Hardy would be a manipulation, rather than a natural response. The joy of the thrush survives to the end of the poem precisely because it is left alone, because it is allowed to remain incongruous. The aged thrush acquires not meaning but heroism, and our aesthetic response to the whole, which is finally our response to the attitude of the speaker in the last stanza, is founded upon a sense of temptations heroically resisted and suffering laconically undergone.

Despite his anti-Romantic deflations and his apparently relentless schematizing, Hardy is at heart the least analytical of poets. In him, the tendency to assimilate and transform, to make something of what he sees, is less pronounced than in any of the Romantics (even Keats), and his poems are accordingly noninvocational—they leave their readers and their subjects alone in ways that those of his forebears do not. The Romantic crisis of perception and identity is seldom evident in Hardy. He accepted, in fact needed, the limits which they, whether quietly or frenetically, sought to disbelieve. The result is a transformation of the nature and possibilities of poetry which accounts for the blend of restraint and desire, of strength and sentiment, which is characteristic of Hardy. Perkins sees the poetic retreat in "The Darkling Thrush" as a kind of humility or loss of confidence: "the speaker hardly feels able to challenge the rightness of the bird's joy, but in humility and wistful nostalgia states his inability to share it; and the poem presents not a speaker who asserts a mournful pessimism as a necessary reflection from the facts of life, but rather one who feels himself to be incapable of seeing whole, being in some way stunted and incomplete."[8] This sense of diminution, this acquiescence in the limitations of knowledge, is a constant feature of Hardy's poetry and novels. Dozens of poems turn on dramatic contrasts of awarenesss involving either two people, as in "That Moment"—

The tragedy of that moment
Was deeper than the sea,
When I came in that moment
And heard you speak to me!

What I could not help seeing
Covered life as a blot;
Yes, that which I was seeing,
And knew that you were not.
[CP778]

or the same person at different times—as in the wonderfully elusive "The Self-Unseeing," in which Hardy recalls the joy of a family gathering, a joy made poignant by the subsequent death of his father:[9]

Here is the ancient floor,
Footworn and hollowed and thin,
Here was the former door
Where the dead feet walked in.

She sat here in her chair,
Smiling into the fire;
He who played stood there,
Bowing it higher and higher.

Childlike, I danced in a dream;
Blessings emblazoned that day;
Everything glowed with a gleam;
Yet we were looking away!
[CP152]

In these two poems, as in "The Darkling Thrush," blissful ignorance and painful awareness are held in suspension. Hardy hovers over the ignorance of the living and the oblivion of the dead, knowing and remembering. He is neither visionary nor prophet, but executor, and his humility and concern in the face of our troubles and limitations lend to his work a kind of accessible humaneness which is not always so obvious in the more ambitious Romantics. His characteristic acceptance and exploitation of isolation and ignorance have, however, a negative side, on which Blake's *Europe* provides the best gloss:

12

Five windows light the cavern'd Man; thro' one he
                                    breathes the air;
Thro' one, hears music of the spheres; thro' one,
                                    the eternal vine
Flourishes, that he may receive the grapes; thro' one
                                    can look.
And see small portions of the eternal world that
                                    ever groweth;
Thro' one, himself pass out what time he please,
                                    but he will not;
For stolen joys are sweet, & bread eaten in secret
                                    pleasant.

That is, Hardy is something of a voyeur, thought the neurotic and self-titillating aspects of his poetic stance can easily be overemphasized. In his aptly titled book *Distance and Desire*, J. Hillis Miller, noting Hardy's instinct for "passive withdrawal" and his fascination with the "motif of spying," underscores his distance from life:

> It will be remembered that a spontaneous withdrawal of the mind into onlooking separation is the beginning of his own adventure in life. Frightened by the glare and garish rattle around him, he moves to the periphery and watches quietly from a safe position of disengagement. This disengagement seems to lie behind Hardy's choice of a career as a writer. It also determines the voice and stance of his narrators, that cold detachment and wide vision of all events in time and space which is present from the first words of each novel in the objectivity of the narrative language. His writing, I have argued, is undertaken as a safe means of exploring various kinds of involvement, especially that fascinated pursuit of another person which is his concept of love. Writing is a secure way of gambling with life, a way in which it appears that he cannot lose, whichever side of the coin falls uppermost.[10]

"Passive withdrawal" and "cold detachment" certainly characterize one kind of vision in Hardy, and since it is the vision usually found at the beginnings of his novels (where characters emerge from a vast natural backdrop) and at the ends (when all the facts and their consequences are known) it is tempting to see it as definitive. It is a vision of human insignificance and the power of fate, but at least half of Hardy believes in human possibility, and nearly all of him asserts that though our humanity is little enough it is *all* that is significant. Miller's book is undeniably important, but the Hardy who emerges from it is weaker and more neurotic than the one who fills the pages of *The Collected Poems*. Hardy, for all his detachment, never "withdrew" from writing, or from caring.

When in his great "Ode" Wordsworth addressed the visionary child with,

> Full soon thy Soul shall have her earthly freight,
> And custom lie upon thee with a weight,
> Heavy as frost, and deep almost as life!

he intuited the forces which would destroy him. Wordsworth was a poet of the finding of an identity, and when identity found him, it found him no longer a poet. The child, however, grew up to be Thomas Hardy. The "weight" under which Wordsworth was eventually to bow, the terrible inevitability of identity, is for Hardy at least a mixed blessing—it inhibits lyric flight, but it gives him a leverage and solidity, an overwhelming sense of home and self. It is this weight which Hardy lifts in his metrically laborious lines, in his deliberate violations of his established level of diction, and in his changes of distance from his subjects. It is a gravity which holds him, limits him, diminishes him, but which makes every graceful movement possible. It is the inevitability of the self, the mechanical necessity of being, against which he conceives his longing for the infinite chances and possibilities of life and lives. If it accounts for his habitual coldness, detachment, and isolation, it also gives him a place to stand while he reaches out to other lives. Its very inescapability drives him to seek out the possibilities of involvement.

Hardy, like the Romantics, defines himself in relation to what he is not, but his more burdensome sense of identity precludes manipulations and invocations on the Romantic scale. It is through constant, minute movements—little rebellions against gravity, changes in distance and attitude—that he stays in touch with himself. This is evident not only in the nature of his obsessive topics and concerns, but also in his metrical habits and his idiosyncratic diction. Indeed, Hardy's matter and method are so well adapted to each other from the first that one is tempted to see in their congruence a reason for his lack of "development" as a poet. For the moment, however, we shall be concerned with the conflict of necessity and possibility as a recurrent thematic and emotional concern.

Hardy knows well enough, at least for his limited purposes, who he is, and his strength is that he does not rest with that knowledge, despite a very fundamental tendency to withdraw, to surrender to almighty necessity. Like Tennyson's Tithonus, he is in danger of being consumed by his own immortality, but if a fatalist is one who escapes responsibility for what he is on deterministic grounds, then Hardy is not a fatalist, for he repeatedly forces himself to confront the specter of wasted and unfulfilled life. For the settled and submissive man, the most terrible question is what might have been, and it is this question which Hardy asks again and again. He continually torments himself with the arbitrariness of what he is, with the paralyzing vista of infinite possibility. His poetry is an obsessive investigation of desire, and a perpetual elegy on the death of possibility. He teaches us not what we are, but how to endure what we have become.

These concerns are strikingly evident in the militantly odd "The Temporary the All," which Hardy selected to introduce *Wessex Poems*, his first volume of verse:

> Change and chancefulness in my flowering youthtime,
> Set me sun by sun near to one unchosen;
> Wrought us fellowlike, and despite divergence,
>     Fused us in friendship.
>
> "Cherish him can I while the true one forthcome—
> Come the rich fulfiller of my prevision;
> Life is roomy yet, and the odds unbounded."
>     So self-communed I.
>
> 'Thwart my wistful way did a damsel saunter,
> Fair, albeit unformed to be all-eclipsing;
> "Maiden meet," held I, "till arise my forefelt
>     Wonder of women."
>
> Long a visioned hermitage deep desiring,
> Tenements uncouth I was fain to house in:
> "Let such lodging be for a breath-while," thought I,
>     "Soon a more seemly.

"Then high handiwork will I make my life-deed,
Truth and Light outshow; but the ripe time pending,
Intermissive aim at the thing sufficeth."
　　Thus I. . . . But lo, me!

Mistress, friend, place, aims to be bettered straightway,
Bettered not has Fate or my hand's achievement;
Sole the showance those of my onward earth-track—
　　Never transcended!

It is possible to see a peculiar appropriateness in this stanza without wishing that Hardy had used it more often. In general, meters which deviate wildly from the iambic norm (excluding those which fall easily into jog-trot) are likely to express restraint, perhaps merely because they frustrate our expectations. This particular poem makes its reader wish for relaxation, a wish which is only intensified by the alliterative and metrically tense short lines at the end of each stanza. The frustrations and tensions, however, build, and are, indeed, "never transcended." The wrong-headedly abstract diction contributes to the sense of something withheld, of reluctance, in that it creates (almost paradoxically) an impression of terseness—"The Temporary the All," like so many of Hardy's poems, sounds like an abridgment of a longer poem. Swinburne, in his "Sapphics," which Paul Zietlow plausibly adduces as Hardy's model (while perhaps implausibly preferring Hardy's version), also seems to feel the potential for hardness and reluctance in sapphics[11]:

> All the night sleep came not upon my eyelids,
> Shed not dew, nor shook nor unclosed a feather,
> Yet with lips shut close and with eyes of iron
> 　　Stood and beheld me.

"The Temporary the All" is not one of Hardy's very best poems, but it embodies the impressive restraint so crucial to poems such as "The Darkling Thrush." Both poems turn on dramatic contrasts of awareness, and assert not the transcendence of any one perspective but only its finality or inevitability. The speaker in "The Temporary the All" is irrevocably what he is, but he can say no more than this. He is only one of the many people he could have been, and he forces himself to see how easily he could have been something else. The poem presents both the short and long views of

16

events, and the strange meter supports each in turn. On one hand, it has a tentativeness which arises from its persistent violation of our expectations. On the other, its elaborate slowness demands our involvement in the individual stanzas. The terrible restraint and difficulty of the whole performance are clues that the poem deals with what is for Hardy the most painful of issues. It is in fact a challenge of the basis of identity, of the inevitability of inevitability.

Hardy's poems usually fail from excessive strength or excessive sentimentality, and this one is repressed to a maddening degree. It is too tense, too summary, too bound up in its metrical straitjacket. It provides no adequate release for the myriad emotional tensions which it calls into being. Hardy was apparently self-conscious about his initial large-scale public appearance in verse, and one is tempted to surmise that it was precisely the defensive stoicism of "The Temporary the All" which earned it pride of place in *Wessex Poems*.

The third poem in the volume, "Hap," also shows Hardy mired in singleness but refusing to find the easy way out (or rather the easy way to stay in):

> If but some vengeful god would call to me
> From up the sky, and laugh: "Thou suffering thing,
> Know that thy sorrow is my ecstasy,
> That thy love's loss is my hate's profiting!"
>
> Then would I bear it, clench myself, and die,
> Steeled by the sense of ire unmerited;
> Half-eased in that a Powerfuller than I
> Had willed and meted me the tears I shed.
>
> But not so. How arrives it joy lies slain,
> And why unblooms the best hope ever sown?
> —Crass Casualty obstructs the sun and rain,
> And dicing Time for gladness casts a moan . . .
> These purblind Doomsters had as readily strown
> Blisses about my pilgrimage as pain.
>
> [CP7]

This is one of Hardy's most frequently anthologized poems, but it is very far from his best—much further than "The Temporary the

All.'' The discipline of the sonnet is mere play, in comparison to his own sense of form, and what is a "narrow room" for Wordsworth is a veritable darkling plain for Hardy. Banging around in the form, he soon falls into conventional rhythms, especially in the sestet, where he seems bewildered in an excess of space. This may be an object lesson on Hardy's need for limits.

Though Hardy's inability to be comfortable in the sonnet form accounts for some of the weakness of the poem, its most serious fault is its tendency toward sermonizing. In this it may be fatally influenced by Wordsworth's sonnets. When Hardy trundles out The Capitalized, he writes at a distance from his feelings, and the poem rarely survives the resultant slackness. His favorite table-thumpers (Immanent Will, Doom, Crass Casualty, etc.) are not entirely effective abstractions from the feelings underlying such poems as "The Temporary the All." One side of Hardy is always overburdened by the necessity of the present, while the other challenges it and seeks involvement with other lives, with the way things might have been:

> Calm fell. From Heaven distilled a clemency;
> There was peace on earth, and silence in the sky;
> Some could, some could not, shake off misery:
> The Sinister Spirit sneered: "It had to be!"
> And again the Spirit of Pity whispered, "Why?"
> [CP558]

The appearance of *Wessex Poems* late in 1898, when Hardy was fifty-eight, probably represented for him the resurrection of a possibility long buried under habit, circumstance, and financial necessity. Though his urge to "remake" himself never took the extreme forms of Yeats's, his fires died stubbornly, and he declined noticeably as a poet only after the publication of his greatest achievement, *Moments of Vision,* when he was seventy-seven. Hardy was born to be the last man on earth, and he played the role from the beginning, but the older he grew, and the more fate seemed to have triumphed, the more his desires rebelled. He saved his youth until he really needed it, and it kept him alive, in all senses of the word, for a long time. "I Look into My Glass," which closes *Wessex Poems,* functions with "The Temporary the All" as a frame emphasizing the poet's refusal to accept the inevitable:

> I look into my glass,
> And view my wasting skin,
> And say, "Would God it came to pass
> My heart had shrunk as thin!"
>
> For then, I, undistrest
> By hearts grown cold to me,
> Could lonely wait my endless rest
> With equanimity.
>
> But Time, to make me grieve,
> Part steals, lets part abide;
> And shakes this fragile frame at eve
> With throbbings of noontide.
>
> [CP72]

Underlying Hardy's (and for that matter Tennyson's) work is a tone of muted elegy, a vague sense of loss which both precedes and follows poems, and which often seems to cause them. The emotional genesis of Hardy's poems is often obscured because he has decided how a poem will end before he begins it. In the weaker poems, the end is too obviously the cause of writing and the rest is merely a kind of delaying action or suspense. "A Commonplace Day," however, does not seem to have been written backwards. Its rambling discursiveness, unusual in Hardy, suggests that he started with nothing, or rather with only his characteristic tone of crepuscular regret, and his analysis thereof is all the more significant for our purposes in that it is unforeseen:

> The day is turning ghost,
> And scuttles from the kalendar in fits and furtively,
>     To join the anonymous host
> Of those that throng oblivion; ceding his place, maybe,
>     To one of like degree.
>
>     I part the fire-gnawed logs,
> Rake forth the embers, spoil the busy flames, and lay the ends
>     Upon the shining dogs;
> Further and further from the nooks the twilight's stride extends,
>     And beamless black impends.

Nothing of tiniest worth
Have I wrought, pondered, planned; no one thing asking
blame or praise,
Since the pale, corpse-like birth
Of this diurnal unit, bearing blanks in all its rays—
Dullest of dull-hued Days!

Wanly upon the panes
The rain slides, as have slid since morn my colourless
thoughts; and yet
Here, while Day's presence wanes,
And over him the sepulchre-lid is slowly lowered and set,
He wakens my regret.

Regret—though nothing dear
That I wot of, was toward in the wide world at his prime,
Or bloomed elsewhere than here,
To die with his decease, and leave a memory sweet, sublime,
Or mark him out in Time . . . .

—Yet, maybe, in some soul,
In some spot undiscerned on sea or land, some impulse rose,
Or some intent upstole
Of that enkindling ardency from whose maturer glows
The world's amendment flows;

But which, benumbed at birth
By momentary chance or wile, has missed its hope to be
Embodied on the earth;
And undervoicings of this loss to man's futurity
May wake regret in me.

[CP104-5]

We may add as a chorus, "So sad, so strange, the days that never were." Here, Hardy grapples with the emotion basic to his poetry. In the end, the specific terms of his analysis are not so important as his general conclusion—that his seemingly baseless sorrow is in fact a lament for that which has "missed its hope to be." Though it will not do to overemphasize a poet's conscious reading of his most deeply habitual feelings, this poem is in a way unguarded. If it is indeed as true to Hardy as it seems, we may conclude that Hardy's challenge to the basis of identity and necessity, his longing for lost chances and possibilities, underlies the very mood of his poetry, and that it is a ghostly presence, active even when invisible.

In the novels and narrative poems, the lyrical longing for lost chances is translated into bizarre plotting, highly contrived ironies, and dependence on coincidence. J. Hillis Miller provides the best summary of the structure of Hardy's novels as a reflection of his intellectual apprehension of his world:

> Like most people in his epoch, Hardy accepts without question a universal principle of causality. Every event, every choice, every experience has its appointed physical cause. His notion of causality is not the Aristotelean or Christian one of an original or final cause. Nor is it the secular version of the Protestant notion of responsibility which appears in George Eliot's early work: the idea of a single act which starts an irremediable chain of effects. Nor is it that more sophisticated notion in *Middlemarch* of a complex web of causes interacting simultaneously. Hardy's image of the total working of the Immanent Will may be of the latter sort, but his image of a single human life is simpler. A life is a chain of small causes, each effect becoming a cause in turn, or being effected anew by a single cause entering from the outside. The whole forms a linear sequence which is the course of a life.[12]

Miller is again taking the long view, and his analysis again leads to an emphasis on the deterministic and ironic aspects of Hardy's vision:

> Many critics have found Hardy's neatly balanced plots offensively artificial, evidence of the concocting mind of the novelist at work in abstraction from the reality of life. To interpret this aspect of his work in such a way is to miss its meaning and to deny him the right to his own peculiar sense of life and of the relation of art to life. Proust was right here. The notion that life is full of unexpected parallelisms, parallelisms which happen spontaneously rather than being the expression of any conscious plan, is a fundamental aspect of Hardy's vision of existence. His carefully proportioned plots express his notion of the ironic incompatibility between a man's conscious intentions, the pattern he wants to give to his life, and the actual design which is surreptitiously being created all the time by a hidden power which

even makes use of a man's free acts to construct its chaste symmetries.[13]

Miller successfully rescues Hardy from critics who invoke a false standard of realism, and he ties Hardy's structural imagination to his sense of life. This is important, and it would be worthwhile to continue on this line of argument. That some readers find Hardy's plots "offensively artificial" is significant, although the phrase suggests that their reaction is more of an objective aesthetic judgment than it really is. Hardy's plots are *upsetting*, even *threatening*. When, for example, Tess's letter of confession is misdirected, the reader is likely to respond by saying, mentally at least, "No, no, this does not *have* to happen." At every turn we are faced with situations which are eminently evitable, which seem fated only in retrospect. We find ourselves dealing with the tragedy of *Othello*, not that of *Hamlet*, and we are likely to be muttering "if only, if only." This kind of tragedy is so hard to take (see Samuel Johnson's reaction to the death of Cordelia in *King Lear*) in part because it is so unnecessary. Though it is easy to see the strict rationalism of Hardy's plotting as a statement about the universe, the very artifice of his chains of events calls attention to their arbitrariness (as the comments of Miller's "many readers" imply). It constantly recalls *what might have been*, and this, as we have seen, is Hardy's constant and passionate concern. This is the short view of the events of Hardy's narratives, and its closeness to the emotional basis of the poetry suggests that some of the vehemence of the criticism of the structure of Hardy's novels is attributable less to high artistic principles than to the real and disturbing threat posed by Hardy's challenge to the basis of identity. We are forced to recognize simultaneously how irrevocably things are what they are and how easily they could have been otherwise. This can be hard knowledge, and Hardy's strength is that he repeatedly makes himself bear it. There is indeed a cold and detached fatalism in Hardy's long view of events, but it is consistently subverted by his valiant preservation of possibilities, his rugged refusal to let old wounds heal.

The paradox of necessity and possibility informs Hardy's somewhat peculiar treatment of human passion. Refusing, even for poetic purposes, to see love as transcendent, or even as a way into the transcendent, he instead views it in terms of limitation—as the choice of a particular person and thus of a particular life. His challenge of the inevitability of identity is usually inseparable from his realization of the arbitrariness of love:

> To feel I might have kissed—
>   Loved as true—
> Otherwhere, nor Mine have missed
>   My life through,
> Had I never wandered near her,
> Is a smart severe—severer
> In the thought that she is nought,
> Even as I, beyond the dells
>   Where she dwells.
>
> [CP14]

For Hardy, love is a chance, and as such it becomes most attractive when it is no longer possible, as in the striking number of poems on love rejuvenated by death. Crushing inevitability galvanizes desire. The strangely compelling "In the Moonlight" provides the best illustration:

> "O lonely workman, standing there
> In a dream, why do you stare and stare
> At her grave, as no other grave there were?
>
> "If your great gaunt eyes so importune
> Her soul by the shine of this corpse-cold moon
> Maybe you'll raise her phantom soon!"
>
> "Why, fool, it is what I would rather see
> Than all the living folk there be;
> But alas, there is no such joy for me!"
>
> "Ah—she was the one you loved, no doubt,
> Through good and evil, through rain and drought,
> And when she passed, all your sun went out?"
>
> "Nay: she was the woman I did not love,
> Whom all the others were ranked above,
> Whom during her life I thought nothing of."
>
> [CP398]

Impossibility becomes reason enough for love, as also in "The Torn Letter," where Hardy destroys what is apparently a fan letter and is unable to recover the name and address of the sender:

V

Uprising then, as things unpriced
 I sought each fragment, patched and mended;
 The midnight whitened ere I had ended
And gathered words I had sacrificed.

VI

But some, alas, of those I threw
 Were past my search, destroyed for ever:
 They were your name and place; and never
Did I regain those clues to you.

VII

I learnt I had missed, by rash unheed,
 My track; that, so the Will decided,
 In life, death, we should be divided,
And at the sense I ached indeed.

VIII

That ache for you, born long ago,
 Throbs on: I never could outgrow it.
 What a revenge, did you but know it!
But that, thank God, you do not know.

[CP295]

The poem is a strange monument to Hardy's war against inevitability, to his desire to live all possible lives, as is his fascination with women he chose to see as inaccessible:

> The girl in the omnibus had one of those faces of marvellous beauty which are seen casually in the streets but never among one's friends. It was perfect in its softened classicality—a Greek face translated into English. Moreover she was fair, and her hair pale chestnut. Where do these women come from? Who marries them? Who knows them?
> [L220]

The other side of Hardy's concern with impossible love is his involuntary shrinking from the achievement of desire. Even as his romance with Emma Lavinia Gifford of St. Juliot, Cornwall, where Hardy was involved in the restoration of her father's church, was proceeding smoothly toward marriage, Hardy titillated himself by imagining disaster in *A Pair of Blue Eyes*. Published in 1873, the year before his marriage, the novel deals with a Cornwall girl, like Emma the daughter of a clergyman, who rejects two versions of Hardy—an architect and a literary man—only to marry an aristocrat and die soon after.

The consequence of conceiving love as a choice necessarily involving the exclusion of possibilities is a strong emphasis on submission to the beloved. Hardy's lovers are usually mismatched, and it is probably significant in this context that Emma Hardy never let him forget that she had married beneath her, and that she would not permit his parents in her home. Those in love with people of a higher social class (Diggory Venn, Gabriel Oak, Marty South—their very names sound alike, and sound suspiciously like "Thomas Hardy") become neo-Elizabethan servant-lovers, caring, hoping, and knowing at a distance. Angel Clare, on the other hand, submits to an ideal of innocence and simplicity which he discovers, or rather creates, in Tess. The threat posed by the narrowness of love drives Hardy's characters to potentially destructive idolatry—they feel a need to make the object of their love mean and be more than he or she possibly can.

The servant-lovers, impossibly isolated beings who watch, care, and manipulate from a position of superior knowledge, are, as Hardy's obvious delight in them suggests, figures for the artist. For Hardy, the poet is neither prophet nor linguistic superman, but rather an invisible lover who notices things:

> When the present has latched its postern behind my
> tremulous stay,
> And the May month flaps its glad green leaves
> like wings,
> Delicate-filmed as new-spun silk, will the neighbours
> say,
> "He was a man who used to notice such things"?
> [CP521]

The poet is characterized by curiosity and concern, by a desire to know about other people, to tell their stories, and to enrich his memories with theirs:

"You were a poet—quite the ideal
  That we all love awhile:
But look at this man snoring here—
He's no romantic chanticleer,
  Yet keeps me in good style.

"He makes no quest into my thoughts,
  But a poet wants to know
What one has felt from earliest days,
Why one thought not in other ways,
  And one's loves of long ago."

                                    [CP356]

The service of Hardy's voracious and caressing memory, which
Miller calls "the safeguarding of the dead,"[14] is in part self-service,
for his refusal to let things be forgotten seems at times to stem from
his own fear of death. Indeed, he flirts with the idea of a second life
in memory:

I

I saw a dead man's finer part
Shining within each faithful heart
Of those bereft. Then said I: "This must be
  His immortality."

II

I looked there as the seasons wore,
And still his soul continuously bore
A life in theirs. But less its shine excelled
  Than when I first beheld.

III

His fellow-yearsmen passed, and then
In later hearts I looked for him again;
And found him—shrunk, alas! into a thin
  And spectral mannikin.

IV

Lastly I ask—now old and chill—
If aught of him remain unperished still;
And find, in me alone, a feeble spark,
  Dying amid the dark.

                                    [CP130]

In general, however, Hardy's cherishing of his subjects (he regularly falls in love with his heroines) must be seen as a preservation of possibility, an empathy with other lives. His love and knowledge are gently possessive, as if in rescuing people from oblivion, in caring for them, he could make their lives a part of his own:

> Never a careworn wife but shows,
>   If a joy suffuse her,
> Something beautiful to those
>   Patient to peruse her,
> Some one charm the world unknows
>   Precious to a muser,
> Haply what, ere years were foes,
>   Moved her mate to choose her.
> [CP132]

The relentless process of remembering and preserving furnishes his life and makes it livable:

> Do they know me, whose former mind
> Was like an open plain where no foot falls,
> But now is as a gallery portrait-lined,
> And scored with necrologic scrawls . . .
> [CP666]

In the end, the emphasis on a second life in memory is superseded by the digestion of character by places, houses, and the landscape, which, after years and volumes of use, begins to take on the qualities of a worn path or a familiar, if not always comfortable, room. The process of remembering begins to become independent of the living, as the past struggles back into the light, back into human awareness. Even the most barren scenes bloom with human memory, and ghosts blur the garish and unpromising outlines of the present.

In Hardy's poetry, the dead represent a seemingly irredeemable pastness, a complete absence of possibility, and they seem to symbolize that part of Hardy which has been crushed under its own inevitability. They are an obsessive concern, for their disappearance is seen as a threat to the living, a closing of doors which provokes Hardy's claustrophobic reaction to inevitability. Though we shall postpone discussion of Hardy's ghosts and his dead until chapter four, we must note here that they are the most bewitching and inaccessible of his lovers, and that he spares no effort to make them live, to assimilate their presence and their possibilities, and to lament their helplessness.

With all this emphasis on Hardy as the poet of possibility, he begins to sound like an apostle of human freedom, which, as nearly everyone recognizes, he is not. His courageous confrontation of the past is counterbalanced by a fear of the future:

> "Who's in the next room?—who?
>     I seem to hear
> Somebody muttering firm in a language new
>     That chills the ear."
> "No: you catch not his tongue who has entered there."
>
> "Who's in the next room?—who?
>     I seem to feel
> His breath like a clammy draught, as if it drew
>     From the Polar Wheel."
> "No: none who breaths at all does the door conceal."
>
> "Who's in the next room?—who?
>     A figure wan
> With a message to one in there of something due?
>     Shall I know him anon?"
> "Yea he; and he brought such; and you'll know him anon."
>                                                    [CP473]

Hardy, when he is least abstract and most himself, considers the future only in terms of death, in terms of its becoming the past. Chances interest him only when they are already lost, and only the terrible weight of inevitability galvanizes his desires. The future, with its infinitely chaotic and unfamiliar possibilities, is fearsome and unmanageably strange. Hardy is above all the poet of things as usual, and his taste for possibility and bizarre incident arises only in opposition to his natural inertia. He is the poet of "mechanic repetition," as he asserts in "Why do I," the closing poem of what he probably expected to be his last volume of verse:

> Why do I go on doing these things?
>     Why not cease?
> Is it that you are yet in this world of welterings

And unease,
And that, while so, mechanic repetitions please?
[CP791]

Hardy caresses words, patterns, places, and lives into familiarity. His first task is to make a home for himself. Only then does he take care to see that it is not too small. He submits to almost architectural limits of space and time, to a muted voice, and to a narrow range of topics and concerns. His sea of faith has withdrawn, and he clings manfully to the rocks, to "great things":

> The dance it is a great thing,
>   A great thing to me,
> With candles lit and partners fit
>   For night-long revelry;
> And going home when day-dawning
>   Peeps pale upon the lea:
> O dancing is a great thing,
>   A great thing to me!
>
> Love is, yea, a great thing,
>   A great thing to me,
> When, having drawn across the lawn
>   In darkness silently,
> A figure flits like one a-wing
>   Out from the nearest tree:
> O love is, yes, a great thing,
>   A great thing to me!
>
> Will these be always great things,
>   Great things to me? . . .
> Let it befall that One will call,
>   "Soul, I have need of thee:"
> What then? Joy-jaunts, impassioned flings,
>   Love, and its ecstasy,
> Will always have been great things,
>   Great things to me!

[CP445]

We have been investigating two sides of a paradox. The self is both ponderously inevitable and infinitely divisible, and its objects are simultaneously distant and intimate. In the end, Hardy's attitude toward great things and other lives is ambivalent. On one hand, he revels in familiarity and possessive love. On the other, he rejects the domestication of otherness, and prefers inaccessibility:

> II
> About my path there flits a Fair,
> Who throws me not a word or sign;
> I'll charm me with her ignoring air,
> And laud the lips not meant for mine.

> IV
> And some day hence, towards Paradise
> And all its blest—if such should be—
> I will lift glad, afar-off eyes,
> Though it contain no place for me.
> [CP222]

These opposing tendencies are apparent not only in separate poems, but also within individual poems, and often in the choice of a single word. They will be examined in detail in a chapter on Hardy's diction, meter, and form, but at this point it is most appropriate to consider Hardy's self-division on a more general level, and to link it to the spirit of the age by examining it in conjunction with that of Robert Browning, whom Richard Howard has called "the great poet of otherness."[15]

# 2
## OTHER LIVES:
## HARDY AND BROWNING

The juxtaposition of the names Hardy and Browning inevitably calls to mind differences, not similarities. Hardy, for all his novelistic forays into the paradoxes of human passion, remains an innocent, though his innocence is that of the theorist rather than that of the primitive. His repertory of sacred objects, patterns, and emotions is perhaps as limited as that of any poet of his stature, and he refuses to wander far from their embrace. His poems, because their sources of delight are few and intense, and because they find it impossible to avoid gratification, quickly find ways to remain short. Hardy specializes in the rediscovery of the familiar, and he substitutes for sustained performance the lifelong variation of a few heartfelt and significant themes. Browning, in contrast, is the most urbane and inclusive of poets, and nothing, human or nonhuman, is alien to his purposes because the alien *is* his purpose. He, too, of course, employs favorite ideas, images, and characters, but he calls them up only to object to them, and uses them as milestones rather than sanctuaries. He has a poised and well-founded trust in the relevance of the irrelevant. A more interested and interesting person than

Hardy, he is not easily bored, and seldom exhibits Hardy's pathological fear of boring his reader. All in all, the attempt to find the common ground of Browning's sprightly, muscular, and rapid intelligence and Hardy's ponderous and vague intuition must at first seem an exercise in the improbable.

Hardy knew Browning and greatly admired his work, but his direct debt to his older contemporary is small, even (and perhaps especially) when it is most obvious. It is not the purpose of this chapter to enlarge the catalogue of Hardy's borrowings and thefts, or to suggest that Browning made use of the four Hardy poems that were published in his lifetime. What the two poets share most conspicuously they discovered independently and inevitably, and this discovery and this fate have large implications for the nature of Victorian poetry in general. Browning and Hardy have in common an implicit myth of their origins in Romanticism, a myth of an impossible innocence and a shattered self. Browning, like Hardy, feels his diminution, and he too gropes his way toward an art of compromise, a difficult accommodation of the conflicting demands of self and other. Both are victims of the paralysis which is the legacy of the dizzying paradoxes of limitation and multiplicity, and their kinship is apparent even in their styles, for both need the solidity of cramped roughed-up poems which seem nailed to the page. This, as we shall see, is the consequence of the struggles and dislocations of form and formlessness, of necessity and possibility.

Hardy's self-image has been hammered out and swallowed by the 1860s, the decade of his earliest surviving poems, and since his willful poetic contraction rarely admits of self-analysis or critical discussion, it is easy to overlook the ubiquitous but quiet effects of his hard-won compromise on his poetic personality. As Samuel Hynes remarks, Hardy did not evolve—he simply narrowed: "The bad early poems are bad Shakespeare or bad Swinburne; the bad late poems are bad Hardy."[1] Though his first volumes contain many vaporous and baggy imitations of Elizabethan and Romantic rhythms, they are dotted with poems in a manner indistinguishable from that which predominates at the end of his life. "Hap," dated 1866 in *Wessex Poems* (1898), is, for all its thunderous iconoclasm, purely Elizabethan in rhythm, while the song "Last Love-Word," dated 189- in *Human Shows* (1925) is written in Hardy's idiosyncratic style, though its language and theme are borrowed from Elizabethan sonnet sequences:

> This is the last; the very, very last!
>     Anon, and all is dead and dumb.
> Only a pale shroud over the past,
>     That cannot be
> Of value small or vast,
>     Love, then to me!
>
> I can say no more: I have even said too much.
>     I did not mean that this should come:
>     I did not know 'twould swell to such—
>         Nor, perhaps, you—
>     When that first look and touch,
>         Love, doomed us two!
>
> [CP704]

The first stanza glances at the situation of Drayton's "Since ther's no helpe" and Wyatt's "My lute awake!" and the second borrows from sonnet 50 of Samuel Daniel's *Delia*, which ends "I say no more, I feare I saide too much," but Hardy has shaped the Elizabethan material, though not without a visible struggle, to his own ends.

Browning, in contrast, starts closer to Shelley, their common ancestor, and his evolutionary struggles, as well-documented as they are unremitting, will illuminate some of the otherwise less visible complications of Hardy's poetry.

For all their differences in temperament, the two poets start from similar emotional premises and similar assumptions about the nature, structure, and relevance of poetry. The bemused and confused speaker of "How It Strikes a Contemporary" discovers in the poet he shadows the same curiosity and concern which Hardy saw as fundamental to the artistic personality:

> You'd come upon his scrutinizing hat,
> Making a peaked shade blacker than itself
> Against the single window spared some house
> Intact yet with its mouldered Moorish work,—
> Or else surprise the ferrel of his stick
> Trying the mortar's temper 'tween the chinks
> Of some new shop a-building, French and fine.

He stood and watched the cobbler at his trade,
The man who slices lemons into drink,
The coffee-roaster's brazier, and the boys
That volunteer to help him turn its winch.
He glanced o'er books on stalls with half an eye,
And fly-leaf ballads on the vender's string,
And broad-edge bold-print posters by the wall.
He took such cognizance of men and things,
If any beat a horse you felt he saw;
If any cursed a woman, he took note. . . .

[B336][2]

If the Hardy who "used to notice such things" (CP521) is not likely
to record lemons, posters, and coffee, he is still one who "wants to
know" (CP356), and if he is more likely to be curious about "one's
Loves of long ago" (CP356), this reflects his profound fascination
with the shape and feel of stories rather than with the thoughts,
objects, and sensations that cluster about the *moments* in a story to
give them character and significance. For both Browning and
Hardy, the poet sees, but he is less a seer than a recorder, as
Browning asserts left-handedly later in "How It Strikes a Contemporary," wryly debunking Shelley's appointment of poets to the
unacknowledged legislatures of the world:

We had among us, not so much a spy,
As a recording chief-inquisitor,
The town's true master if the town but knew!
We merely kept a governor for form,
While this man walked about and took account
Of all thought, said, and acted, then went home,
And wrote it fully to our Lord the King . . .

[B336]

Browning's ironic dismissal of the Shelleyan and supernatural
functions of poetry is no doubt necessary for his psychological
survival in the face of his own diminution, but the other side of his
irony is reverence, and more often than not they are bound
inextricably together, as in "Memorabilia":

Ah, did you once see Shelley plain,
And did he stop and speak to you,
And did you speak to him again?
How strange it seems and new!

34

But you were living before that,
  And also you are living after;
And the memory I stared at—
  My starting moves your laughter!

I crossed a moor, with a name of its own
  And a certain use in the world no doubt,
Yet a hand's-breadth of it shines alone
  'Mid the blank miles round about:

For there I picked up on the heather,
  And there I put inside my breast
A moulted feather, an eagle-feather!
  Well, I forget the rest.

[B195]

This delightful poem, with its movement from idolatry to necessary incoherence, may well be an ancestor of Hardy's "Shelley's Skylark," but where the determined Hardy blunders into preciosity, Browning, always quicker on his feet, sizes up his distance from the Shelleyan, steps away, and makes a poetic virtue out of his necessary helplessness with the brilliantly evasive "Well, I forget the rest."

The myth of diminution is related to the feeling of oldness (which is in turn similar to what Harold Bloom has come to call "belatedness") that recurs in the poetry of Hardy and Browning. Though Browning has the youthfulness which Hardy seldom allows himself, he is often at his best in the elegiac mode, in writing of the old or dying, or of figures burdened with a sense of the lateness or exhaustion of their cultures and styles. The dying St. John of "A Death in the Desert" speaks sadly of the "late days" (B388) of the world, and the Bishop of St. Praxed's erects a tomb around himself with his speech. Karshish, at the dead end of his thought, marvels at the hint of a new age of which he cannot be a part. The late classical Cleon, "stung by the straitness of our life," tries to convince himself that the increasing complexity of man's soul is adequate compensation for the diminution it has suffered:

> Marvel not.
> We of these latter days, with greater mind
> Than our forerunners, since more composite,
> Look not so great, beside their simple way,
> To a judge who only sees one way at once,
> One mind-point and no other at a time,—

Compares the small part of a man of us
With some whole man of the heroic age,
Great in his way—not ours, nor meant for ours.
And ours is greater, had we skill to know . . .
[B359]

Even the energetic Blougram sees himself as living in a ''late time of day'' or ''the tail of time,'' and he is echoed in *The Ring and the Book* by the Pope, who labors under old age and the weight of a vast tradition:

Paul—'tis a legend—answered Seneca,
But that was in the day-spring; noon is now,
We have got too familiar with the light.
Shall I wish back once more that thrill of dawn?
When the whole truth-touched man burned up, one fire?
[B569]

Given this common concern with the dead ends of necessity, we might expect Browning, like Hardy, to be concerned with the resurrection of possibilities, and, to some extent, he is. Poems such as ''Youth and Art'' and ''Dis Aliter Visum'' turn on the lost chances which so fascinate Hardy, as does ''The Statue and the Bust,'' which Hardy twice praises in the *Life* as ''one of his finest'' (L192, 199) precisely because it is the Browning poem he could most easily have written.

On the whole, however, Browning's confrontation with necessity and possibility, with the vagueness and isolation of identity, and the paralyzing chaos of infinite choice, takes place on the levels of style, form, and structure, and accounts, in part, for his resort to the dramatic monologue. Just as Hardy's troubling invocations of lost chances and other lives provide the pain, the perspective of loss, which enables him to stay in touch with a self threatening to fade in the isolation of its eternity, its necessity, so Browning's investigations of the possibilities of characters and objects are the means to a negative redefinition of his ponderous but vague self. Both poets desire to live all their possible lives. J. Hillis Miller says of the early Browning:

Massive substance, a seething diffused energy, a shaping force urging the shapeless bulk toward form—these men

make up the initial Browningesque self and Browningesque
world. To say that the self is a bubbling cauldron of contra-
dictory impulses is the same as to say that the world itself
is a swarming of larvae all dwelling together, crisscrossing,
teeming, crushing one another. But all these forms are possible, not actual. The soul is seething with an immense
power of life, but so far is not actually anything or anybody. As Charles Du Bos puts it in a brilliant phrase,
Browning's personality is "tout ensemble la plus massive et
la plus poreuse qui fut jamais."[3]

It is a little difficult to imagine how a soul which is not "anything
or anybody" decides to write poetry, much less poetry which is so
consistently identifiable as the product of a particular and highly
individual mind, and though it is not really fair to question an
abstraction which serves so well in Miller's brilliant essay unless one
intends to correct and replace it, some objections must be lodged,
especially since Miller himself attributes to this "nobody" a series
of "desires" and "impulses," words that make no sense when
considered in isolation from the self. Although the real dynamics of
Browning's creative impulse are unclear in Miller's essay, he
correctly identifies the poles of Browning's mind, and points to the
fact that for Browning, as for Hardy, each act of creation is both an
escape from an incomprehensible sameness and an act of limitation
—a terrible, difficult, and temporary compromise between necessity and possibility. What Browning called Shelley's "essay towards
a presentiment of the correspondence of the universe to the deity"
(B1014) was impossible for the two later poets. Though they are both
major poets, they do not seek to write poems which are major (or
absolute or universal) in the received sense. They write, instead,
poems which are deliberately minor, occasional, and particularized.
This, as far as we are concerned, is their great strength, but there is
ample evidence that Browning and Hardy were at least a little
uncomfortable with the compromise necessary for their survival,
that they perceived it as necessary, but as a necessary diminution.

According to Browning, the great enemy of the Shelleyan seer is
self-deception, and the two Victorians joined the force which they
felt unable to defeat. They made self-deception fundamental to the
structure of their verse, following the old maxim "divide and

conquer." That is, Hardy bases his poems on contrasts of awareness, and Browning's dramatic monologues take self-deception both as their theme and their form, for the creation of a character involves deliberate exclusions of the self, a kind of dialectic of remembering and forgetting, of distance and involvement, or of what Browning himself saw as knowledge and love. For both poets, the "not I," the other, the perspective of repressed awareness, is equivalent to the "not all of me," and their poetry arises as much from dissociations and dislocations as from visionary correspondences. In a sense, therefore, the diminution is not only necessary but fortuitous, for though the poems close themselves off from Romantic truth (or rather what Browning and Hardy *saw* as Romantic truth), they also escape the possibility of Romantic error. They elude qualification or criticism on these grounds by qualifying and criticizing themselves, by supplying a double perspective. Both poets, perhaps unconsciously, believe that the Romantic self is founded on an innocence which is impossible for them, and they must therefore make their own innocence, their not-knowing or un-knowing, part of a dialectic. Innocence survives, but it is consistently qualified, and it is this qualification which both enables and limits their poetry.

As a result of this division, Browning and Hardy stand at a distance from even their most personal poems, and the poems themselves contain distances in various gradations—from grim and gratuitous irony (found mostly in Hardy), to incongruity, to gentle irony, to dislocation of perspective, to mere reserve. If Shelley is the divine seer, the exclusions and distances of Browning and Hardy stamp them as something akin to divine jesters. Their jests, of course, are seldom what would be called humorous, and they do not have to be as obvious and irrelevant as some of Hardy's:

> Dora's gone to Ireland
>   Through the sleet and snow:
> Promptly she has gone there
>   In a ship, although
> Why she's gone to Ireland
>   Dora does not know.

38

That was where, yea, Ireland,
　Dora wished to be:
When she felt, in lone times,
　Shoots of misery,
Often there, in Ireland,
　Dora wished to be.

Hence she's gone to Ireland,
　Since she meant to go,
Through the drift and darkness
　Onward labouring, though
That she's gone to Ireland
　Dora does not know.
                    [CP873]

This particular poem merely straddles the fence between incongruity and dull humor, but it is a garish outcropping of Hardy's typical vein. The gods' sports with the characters of his novels, and the gentler incongruities and contrasts of awareness in his poetry all necessarily partake of the jest which arises from the exclusions, manipulations, and concealments which are inescapably his. Browning's Sludge, who is a hoaxer by profession, and who is as brutally and finally undercut as any of his monologists, must nevertheless, at times, be taken seriously as a representative of the poet, and even as a figure *for* the poet, and Blougram, who jests and manipulates obsessively, is still classifying and bewildering interpreters who seek to fix him in some moral continuum. Where deception and self-deception are the rules of the game (and it is, to some extent, a game), jest is the order of the day. The obvious cases shade into the dozens where Browning and his character hoax the reader or themselves. The issue is too complicated for exhaustive discusion at this point, but we may say that the element of jest, like the conscious acts of exclusion to which it is related, is both a way of knowing and a way of hiding, a kind of creation through contraction.

Browning's compromise was forged painfully and at length, and it will now be useful to turn to *Pauline* (1833), his first major effort. No one has failed to notice that this poem was written under the crushing influence of Shelley, who is in fact its major character, but although Shelley is undoubtedly one muse of this footnote to *Alastor* and *Epipsychidion*, many facets of the poem, including the verse movement so decisive for a young poet, accuse Wordsworth of paternity. Looking ahead to the terminology of the essay on Shelley, critics tend to see *Pauline* as Browning's doomed attempt at Shelleyan or "subjective" poetry. Miller calls *Pauline* a version of the "central adventure of romanticism—the attempt to identify oneself with God" and says that it climaxes in "the failure of romantic Prometheanism."[4] *Pauline* is certainly different from Browning's later work, and just as certainly deficient in drama or "objectivity," but if it is subjective it contains seeds not sown by Shelley, and if we are to call it Promethean we must explain away the lack of confidence at its core. This, for example, is the first climax of the poem:

> Thou wilt remember one warm morn when winter
> Crept aged from the earth, and spring's first breath
> Blew soft from the moist hills; the black-thorn boughs,
> So dark in the bare wood, when glistening
> In the sunshine were white with coming buds,
> Like the bright side of a sorrow, and the banks
> Had violets opening from sleep like eyes,
> I walked with thee who knew'st not a deep shame
> Lurked beneath smiles and careless words which sought
> To hide it till they wandered and were mute,
> As we stood listening on a sunny mound
> To the wind murmuring in the damp copse,
> Like heavy breathings of some hidden thing
> Betrayed by sleep; until the feeling rushed
> That I was low indeed, yet not so low
> As to endure the calmness of thine eyes.
> And so I told thee all ...

[B3]

"I told thee all" is hardly Promethean, and it is only the beginning of an uneasy litany of attempted self-exposures which continues with "Still I can lay my soul bare in its fall" (B3), "I strip my mind bare, whose first elements/I shall unveil" (B4), "And I can love nothing—and this dull truth/Has come the last" (B5), and "I will tell/My state as though 'twere none of mine'' (B7). This is curiously passive, and so is the love in the poem as in "And now, my Pauline, I am thine forever" (B10) or the striking prediction of "Porphyria's Lover"—

> How the blood lies upon her cheek, outspread
> As thinned by kisses! only in her lips
> It wells and pulses like a living thing,
> And her neck looks like marble misted o'er
> With love-breath,—a Pauline from heights above,
> Stooping beneath me, looking up—one look
> As I might kill her and be loved the more.
>
> [B10]

or the final paragraph of the poem, where the exhausted Browning falls into the embrace of Shelley to receive life:

> Sun-treader, I believe in God and truth
> And love; and as one just escaped from death
> Would bind himself in bands of friends to feel
> He lives indeed, so, I would lean on thee!
> Thou must be ever with me, most in gloom
> If such must come, but chiefly when I die,
> For I seem, dying, as one going in the dark
> To fight a giant: but live thou forever,
> And be to all what thou hast been to me!
> All in whom this wakes pleasant thoughts of me
> Know my last state is happy, free from doubt
> Or touch of fear. Love me and wish me well.
>
> [B11]

If *Pauline* is Shelleyan, it also reveals the habit of submission which will lead to Browning's art of compromise. Where Shelley asks the muse to speak through him, Browning asks to be protected, to be allowed to speak to the muse. The young Browning imitates not Shelley but his powerlessness in the face of Shelley's power. The limiting muse, a combination of Pauline, God, and Shelley, is for Browning, as for Andrea del Sarto, female (as Browning's Italy is the "woman country, wooed not wed" [B185]) and he submits to her, for the art of compromise is a marriage of voices. Harold Bloom provides the parallel from Browning's private life: "Browning's experience of what Blake called the Female Will had been confined largely to his mother and his wife, neither of whom he had shaped to his mind; rather he had yielded to both."[5] In fact, the Browning of *Pauline* is not trying to "identify" himself with anything—he cannot even identify himself. Instead, he tries to give himself away—to Pauline, to God, to Shelley—as if the act of giving and the necessity of choice would limit and shape his vagueness and galvanize one who "can love nothing":

> O God, where do they tend—these struggling aims?
> What would I have? What is this "sleep" which seems
> To bound all? Can there be a "waking" point
> Of crowning life? The soul would never rule;
> It would be first in all things, it would have
> Its utmost pleasure filled, but, that complete,
> Commanding, for commanding, sickens it.
> The last point I can trace is—rest beneath
> Some better essence than itself, in weakness;
> This is "myself," not what I think I should be...
>
> [B 9]

The "giving away" is never very convincing, especially in the cases of God and Pauline, for the discovery that Browning makes about his version of Romanticism is that all is nothing, that in attempting to give all of ourselves we give nothing. He says "Water is beautiful, but not like air" (B9), and air is indeed the element of the poem. The poet of air, of everything and nothing, has no handle on himself, and the idols of air cannot embrace him.

The passage which is by consensus the intellectual crux of the poem does exhibit a kind of modified Prometheanism:

> I am made up of an intensest life,
> Of a most clear idea of consciousness
> Of self, distinct from all its qualities,
> From all affections, passions, feelings, powers;
> And thus far it exists, if tracked in all:
> But linked, in me, to self-supremacy,
> Existing as a centre to all things,
> Most potent to create and rule and call
> Upon all things to minister to it;
> And to a principle of restlessness

Which would be all, have, see, know, taste, feel all—
This is myself; and I should thus have been
Though gifted lower than the meanest soul.

[B4-5]

As W. David Shaw points out, however, "To express intensity the speaker repeats the word "all" four times. His language half congeals into excited stammering, then breaks down into ecstatic "word-heaps." Despite *Pauline*'s lavish use of punctuation, including seventy-one exclamation points, Browning has failed to solve the difficult problem of expressing intensity in poetry."[6] Browning, in other words, tries to meet the self and reality head on, all for all, and has not yet learned that his only approach is through a descent to the strength and limitation of the particular ("for love/Perforce receives its object from the earth," [B8]) and to the strength and limitation of the divided self. Langbaum comments:

> Browning's poetry before 1842 suggests by the manner of its failure the kind of precedent that lay behind the dramatic monologue, and the kind of problem that remained for the dramatic monologue to solve. His first published work, *Pauline* (1833) is the poem in which he too much revealed himself. It is transparently autobiographical.... It was of *Pauline* that John Stuart Mill said: "The writer seems to me possessed with a more intense and morbid self-consciousness than I ever knew in any sane human being"—a criticism Browning took so to heart that he would not allow *Pauline* to be published again until 1867 ... he is reported to have said in his old age that "his early poems were so transparent in their meaning as to draw down upon him the ridicule of the critics, and that, boy as he was, this ridicule and censure stung him into quite another style of writing."[7]

This, however, is only half of the story. Browning says not that his early poems were "transparently autobiographical" but that their *meaning* is transparent—*Pauline* is a film of clichés. Though in one sense Browning "too much revealed himself," in another sense he revealed nothing at all. In either case, his embarrassment is understandable, but, poetically speaking, it is perhaps more important that he found his means of expression inadequate than that he worried about expressing too much, though for Browning the two problems are nearly identical.

In 1852, with *Pauline, Paracelsus, Dramatic Romances and Lyrics, Sordello*, and three dramas behind him, Browning attempted a diagnosis of his condition in an essay on Shelley which was written to preface a collection of newly discovered letters. The letters were forgeries and the volume was never published. The essay on Shelley, "the poet of loftier vision," speaks of the necessary alternation of what Browning calls "subjective" and "objective" poets:

> There is a time when the general eye has, so to speak, absorbed its fill of the phenomena around it, whether spiritual or material, and desires rather to learn the exacter significance of what it possesses than to receive any augmentation of what is possessed. Then is the opportunity for the poet of loftier vision to lift his fellows, with their half-apprehensions, up to his own sphere, by intensifying the import of details and rounding the universal meaning. The influence of such an achievement will not soon die out. A tribe of successors (Homerides), working more or less in the same spirit, dwell on his discoveries and reinforce his doctrine; till, at unawares, the world is found to be subsisting wholly on the shadow of a reality, on sentiments diluted from passions, on the tradition of a fact, the convention of a moral, the straw of last year's harvest. Then is the imperative call for the appearance of another sort of poet, who shall at once replace this intellectual rumination of food swallowed long ago, by a supply of fresh and living swathe; getting at new substance by breaking up the assumed wholes into parts of independent and unclassed value, careless of the unknown laws for recombining them (it will be the business of yet another poet to suggest those hereafter), prodigal of objects for men's outer sight; shaping for their uses a new and different creation from the last, which it displaces by the right of life over death,—to endure until, in the inevitable process, its very sufficiency to itself shall require at length an exposition of its affinity to something higher ...
>
> [B1009–10]

The Browning of *Pauline* is indeed "subsisting wholly on the shadow of a reality, on sentiments diluted from passions," but the alternation which Browning describes here in historical terms is in fact an intuition of his own psychological or poetic processes, as he implies when he says of the subjective and objective faculties that "A mere running in of the one faculty upon the other is, of course, the ordinary circumstance. Far more rarely it happens that either is found so decidely prominent and superior as to be pronounced comparatively pure..." (B1009). The lesson of *Pauline* is that a failure of one of the faculties is inevitably accompanied by a failure in the other, and that some kind of fusion or realignment is necessary. Browning's art must be based on compromise, and that is the position which is developed in his next major work, *Paracelsus* (1835).

*Paracelsus* is hardly better than *Pauline*, but relentless self-critic that he is, Browning is at least more conscious of his problems, and he begins to work them out theoretically, if not practically. This closet drama serves equally well as a critical commentary on *Pauline* or a pretext for the essay on Shelley. It is based on the unbearably clear dramatic opposition of Paracelsus ("I am he that aspired to KNOW," [B23]) and Aprile ("I would LOVE infinitely, and be loved," [B23]). The happily married Festus and Michal serve as chorus, compromise, and voice of moderation. Love becomes the equivalent of submission to the particular, and Aprile, love's spokesman, is a poet, but not *the* poet. This distinction is reserved for the projected fusion of Aprile and Paracelsus, who are "halves of one dissevered world" (B25). Loving, but powerless and dazzled, Aprile is overwhelmed by the multiplicity of possibility, and he dies:

> But, master, poet, who hast done all this,
> How didst thou 'scape the ruin whelming me?
> Didst thou, when nerving thee to this attempt,
> Ne'er range thy mind's extent, as some wide hall,
> Dazzled by shapes that filled its length with light,
> Shapes clustered there to rule thee, not obey,
> That will not wait thy summons, will not rise
> Singly, nor when thy practised eye and hand
> Can well transfer their loveliness, but crowd
> By thee forever, bright to thy despair?
> Didst thou ne'er gaze on each by turns, and ne'er

Resolve to single out one, though the rest
Should vanish, and to give that one, entire
In beauty, to the world; forgetting, so,
Its peers, whose number baffles mortal power?
And, this determined, wast thou ne'er seduced
By memories and regrets and passionate love,
To glance one more farewell? and did their eyes
Fasten thee, brighter and more bright, until
Thou couldst but stagger back unto their feet,
And laugh that man's applause or welfare ever
Could tempt thee to forsake them? Or when years
Had passed and still their love possessed thee wholly,
When from without some murmur startled thee
Of darkling mortals famished for one ray
Of thy so-hoarded luxury of light,
Didst thou ne'er strive even yet to break those spells
And prove thou couldst recover and fulfil
Thy early mission, long ago renounced,
And to that end, select some shape once more?
And did not mist-like influences, thick films,
Faint memories or the rest that charmed so long
Thine eyes, float fast, confuse thee, bear thee off,
As whirling snow-drifts blind a man who treads
A mountain ridge, with guiding spear, through storm?
[B24–25]

When Aprile chooses a particular, he is assailed by the multiplicity of possibility. His choice becomes a necessity and he is seized by the indescribable longing to be what he is not. Paracelsus, on the other hand, is knowledge and power without love. He is not swept away but is instead emptied out by his own Prometheanism, defeated by the vacuum of necessity. He learns, however, what the poet of *Pauline* only sensed—that all is nothing. He dies imagining the reconciliation of his faculties with those of Aprile:

> Let men
> Regard me, and the poet dead long ago
> Who loved too rashly, and shape forth a third
> And better-tempered spirit, warned by both:
> As from the over-radiant star too mad
> To drink the life-springs, beamless thence itself—
> And the dark orb which borders the abyss,

46

Ingulfed in icy night,—might have its course,
A temperate and equidistant world.

[B48]

In *Paracelsus*, Browning has broken the bewildered poet of
*Pauline* into two components. Paracelsus inherits his fascination
with the "all," and upon Aprile is bestowed his characteristic
submissiveness. If we accept Browning's reading of his own situation, we cannot see his evolution as proceeding from subjective to
objective. We must instead premise a radical dislocation of both
faculties—if they are at all separable—for the extremes of both
selflessness and selfishness seem to generate the same emptiness,
vertigo, and vagueness. Failures in the subjective and objective
modes are inextricably intertwined, and it is senseless to speak of
either in isolation from the other.

*Sordello* (1840) is by far the most admirable of these three early
poems, but it is so vast, so full of ironic quicksands, that its exact
significance for Browning's evolution is elusive. The character of
Sordello is an attempt to assume Paracelsus and Aprile into one
gigantic, complex, historical figure. In his re-vision of his own
poetic growth, Browning develops a conception of the simultaneous
independence and interdependence of the self and its objects:

> ficklest king,
> Confessed those minions!—eager to dispense
> So much from his own stock of thought and sense
> As might enable each to stand alone
> And serve him for a fellow; with his own,
> Joining the qualities that just before
> Had graced some older favorite.

[B80]

Just as the objects must be both humanly comprehensible and
self-sustaining, so the self must find its place on the shifting ground
between the demands of necessity and the attractions of possibility:

> "To need become all natures, yet retain
> The law of my own nature—to remain
> Myself, yet yearn . . . as if that chestnut, think,
> Should yearn for this first larch-bloom crisp and pink,

47

Or those pale fragrant tears where zephyrs stanch
March wounds along the fretted pine-tree branch!

[B93]

*Sordello*, for all its obscurity, is transparent in the sense that Browning, if not his reader, is too much aware of what he is doing. His argument never yields finally either to the saving irrelevance of the particular or to the saving familiarity of the self, and the legendary opacity of the poem is defensive rather than functionally insoluble.

No examination of Browning's evolution, however minute, can account for his jump from *Sordello*, with its one confused perspective masquerading as many, to *Pippa Passes* (1841), so breathtaking in its clarity, despite, or rather because of, its radical discontinuities. His three early attempts to record the progress of a soul are versions of the Romantic quest, but they are simultaneously mechanized and confused becuase the quest is, for Browning, necessarily transparent. He cannot manage it unless, as in "Childe Roland to the Dark Tower Came," he backs into it, unless he admits both that he knows where he is going and that he is going nowhere—that the whole quest is written backwards from the end and that it becomes a jest as past approaches present. It is almost as if Browning needed the divisions, dislocations, and coincidences of *Pippa* to woo him from the all which is nothing, from the analytical mockery of Prometheanism, to the little which is something indeed. At this point, he has made his compromise, and it is only a short step to the dramatic monologues in which he debates with himself its limitations and possibilities.

Browning's compromise is neither so easy nor so final that he can accept it without reservations, and he often muses on what now seems his fate. Among his favorite characters are minor artists laboring within bounds analogous to those he has been forced to impose upon himself, and though these particular monologues are by no means reducible to parables on poetry, their obsessive concerns serve to illuminate Browning's sense of his art. The poles of the debate shift and fuse, but it is nevertheless possible to detect the poet feeling out his role.

One of the earliest of these poems is "Pictor Ignotus," which deals with a painter who not only wills himself into minority, but

48

who also, like Cleon, Karshish, Blougram, and others, finds himself in a cultural cul-de-sac. He is old and his style is old. Younger and more expressive painters are conquering the territory of the heart while he reproduces

> These endless cloisters and eternal isles
> With the same series, Virgin, Babe and Saint,
> With the same cold calm beautiful regard ...
>
> [B342]

At first, this restraint seems to be a matter of chance:

> Never did fate forbid me, star by star,
> To outburst on your night with all my gift
> Of fires from God: nor would my flesh have shrunk
> From seconding my soul...
>
> [B341]

We soon learn, however, that necessity, or rather its prime minister, fear, has a hand in the "choice":

> Oh, thus to live, I and my picture, linked
> With love about, and praise, till life should end,
> And then not go to heaven, but linger here,
> Here on my earth, earth's every man my friend,—
> The thought grew frightful, 't was so wildly dear!
> But a voice changed it. Glimpses of such sights
> Have scared me, like the revels through a door
> Of some strange house of idols at its rites!
> This world seemed not the world it was before:
> Mixed with my loving trusting ones, there trooped
> ...Who summoned those cold faces that begun
> To press on me and judge me? Though I stooped
> Shrinking as from the soldiery a nun,
> They drew me forth, and spite of me ... enough!
>
> [B341–42]

In the end, we are left with one statement, and left to decide whether it is a confession or a rationalization: "at least no merchant traffics in my heart." Is this artist justified in his repression of himself? Does fear keep him from being a great artist? Or is his fear really the fear that he cannot be a great artist in any style, and is he protecting himself against the knowledge of his inevitable minority?

It would be difficult to define this painter in the terms of the essay on Shelley. Is he, in his purposeful exclusion of the self and its passions from his work, in his insistence upon the "cold calm beautiful regard," an objective artist? Or is he a defeated subjective artist "subsisting wholly on the shadow of a reality," feeding on the insights of earlier painters. Though the second alternative is initially more convincing, both must be taken into the final accounting. Both of the faculties are dislocated, and the deformation is wrought by a fear which Browning clearly associates with sexual timidity. It is a fear *both* of the self and of the particular. There is danger in the act of opening which the artist must suffer. There is strength in his equally vital contraction, but the extreme of this contraction is the vagary of escapist quiescence, a vagary which in the end denies the self as thoroughly as it denies its objects. It is less important that Browning "identifies" himself with either side of the argument than that he sees fit to depict the artist's dilemmas in these terms, and that a sense of limitation and frustration, of diminution, is central to the poem.

Sexual timidity is not, or not obviously, the problem of "Fra Lippo Lippi," and Lippo himself is so ebullient and convincing that it is hard to see that there is another side to the question he raises. His garrulousness, however, shades into overkill, and if he more than convinces the reader of the excusability of his foray into the Italian spring, he does not seem to convince himself of the propriety of what his excursion *represents* for his art. For though Lippo seems completely reconciled to his immersion in life, it is only because he conveniently displaces his anxieties (the same anxieties displayed in "Pictor Ignotus") onto the gray authority figures of his apprenticeship:

> I'm my own master, paint now as I please—
> Having a friend, you see, in the Corner-house!
> Lord, it's fast holding by the rings in front—
> Those great rings serve more purposes than just
> To plant a flag in, or tie up a horse!
> And yet the old schooling sticks, the old grave eyes
> Are peeping o'er my shoulder as I work,

The heads shake still—"It's art's decline, my son!
You're not of the true painters, great and old ..."

[B344]

Part of Lippo really believes in this decline or diminution, and the
moral is that no one "paints as he pleases" because no one can be
absolutely certain what pleases him. Despite his protestations to the
contrary, Lippo, like the pseudo-Prometheans, worries that he may
be sucked into the vortex of the fleshly particular, that through his
submission to the possibilities of life he may lose its essence and his
own identity. He is *not* his own master because he is still in
rebellion against his own fears. He yearns for certainty:

> all I want's the thing
> Settled forever one way. As it is,
> You tell too many lies and hurt yourself:
> You don't like what you only like too much,
> You do like what, if given at your word,
> You find abundantly detestable.
> For me, I think I speak as I was taught;
> I always see the garden and God there
> A-making man's wife: and my lesson learned,
> The value and significance of flesh,
> I can't unlearn ten minutes afterwards.

[B344]

Lippo's attribution of his confusion to his social conformity is, of
course, an oversimplification. It is in fact the result of a genuine
and inescapable self-division, and he is compelled to rationalize his
interest in the human body in the same terms Browning uses to
justify his fascination with the individual human character. Still,
Lippo, in contrast to Andrea del Sarto and the painter of "Pictor
Ignotus," is a live artist. Accordingly, his compromise is dynamic,
and he does not allow himself to find the fatal certainty he seeks.
His formulations, like Browning's, are only momentary crystallizations. In a poetry of divided awareness, all approximations of
certainty gather into themselves the element of jest or self-deception and become mere rationalizations, but Lippo's vitality tran-
scends both his rationalizations and his misgivings.

It would be fairly easy to confuse Lippo with Browning, but

51

though no one would make that mistake in the case of Andrea del Sarto, it is, paradoxically, the latter who is the more accurate mirror of Browning's personal predicament. In a sense this is not paradoxical at all—it is typical—for the closer Browning gets to himself, the further he steps away. Andrea is another in the line of diminished, late, and limited artists:

> A common grayness silvers everything,—
> All in a twilight, you and I alike
> —You, at the point of your first pride in me
> (That's gone you know),—but I, at every point;
> My youth, my hope, my art, being all toned down
> To yonder sober pleasant Fiesole.

> [B346]

The art of this "faultless painter" is "silver-gray/Placid and perfect." These are the last words we would use to characterize Browning's writing, but Browning's capacity for devious displacements is immeasurable, and here he is more worried about the problem of limitation than about its specific results. In an odd sense, Browning too is faultless, for he sees his poetic enterprise as a low-risk venture. In rejecting visionary truth, he denies the possibility of visionary self-deception—he cannot be right or wrong; he can only be *characteristic*, and the dramatic monologue is a compromise with singularity. It is a marriage with the other analogous to Andrea's submission to his wife, a marriage which both enables and limits art. Browning, whether consciously or unconsciously, laments his necessary act of contraction, his failure to be all, his compromise with a limited kind of perfection:

> This low-pulsed forthright craftsman's hand of mine.
> Their works drop groundward, but themselves, I know,
> Reach many a time a heaven that's shut to me,
> Enter and take their place there sure enough,
> Though they come back and cannot tell the world.
> My works are nearer heaven, but I sit here.
> The sudden blood of these men! at a word—
> Praise them, it boils, or blame them, it boils too.
> I, painting from myself and to myself,
> Know what I do, am unmoved by men's blame
> Or their praise either. Somebody remarks

Morello's outline there is wrongly traced,
His hue mistaken; what of that? or else,
Rightly traced and well ordered; what of that?
Speak as they please, what does the mountain care?
Ah, but a man's reach should exceed his grasp,
Or what's a heaven for? All is silver-gray
Placid and perfect with my art: the worse!

[B346]

The relationship of this kind of art to Browning's own is by no means direct or unambiguous, but the "objective" artist, as a "fashioner" rather than a "seer," is more of a craftsman than the "subjective" artist who "fails ... occasionally in art, only to succeed in the highest art" (B1011). Thus Browning forces a seemingly unlikely parallel between his colorful, low-risk character-izations and the productions of the colorless "perfect" artist. As Browning says in his essay, the subjective and objective faculties are rarely evident in pure form (Shelley's "objective" works, for example, are *Julian and Maddalo* and *The Cenci*), and the dramatic monologues reveal not his preference for one or the other but the tension between them. Consequently, it would be just as correct to take, as Browning also does, the opposite view, and to say that his rough-hewn, noisy, and decidedly unharmonious character sketches are actually the productions of a careless craftsman whose heart is in the right place, but, again, the poet's "opinion," which would in any case be suspect, is less important than his tendency to conceive art in terms of this particular dialectic. Browning manages to find himself on both sides of his idiosyncratic variant of the doctrine of the imperfect. This is a sign, for us and for him, that he is alive. In contrast, Andrea's main fault is that he has settled with, and in, himself:

I am grown peaceful as old age to-night.
I regret little, I would change still less.
Since there my past life lies, why alter it?

[B348]

When carried to extremes, the refusal of Browning and Hardy to accept their own inevitable narrowings is adolescent and even voyeuristic, but Andrea's fervent embrace of his limitations leads to petrifaction. He has displaced his failures onto his wife, and he makes his choice into necessity:

> But all the play, the insight and the stretch—
> Out of me, out of me! And wherefore out?
> Had you enjoined them on me, given me soul,
> We might have risen to Rafael, I and you!
> Nay, Love, you did give all I asked, I think—
> More than I merit, yes, by many times.
> But had you—oh, with the same perfect brow,
> And perfect eyes, and more than perfect mouth,
> And the low voice my soul hears, as a bird
> The fowler's pipe, and follows to the snare—
> Had you, with these the same, but brought a mind!
> Some women do so.
>
> [B347]

This is a rationalization, and Andrea admits in another context what he almost admits here—that his limitations are internal, are only symbolized by Lucrezia:

> A good time, was it not, my kingly days?
> And had you not grown restless . . . but I know—
> 'T is done and past; 'twas right, my instinct said;
> Too live the life grew, golden and not gray,
> And I'm the weak-eyed bat no sun should tempt
> Out of the grange whose four walls make his world.
> How could it end in any other way?
>
> [B347]

Consequently, Andrea's final and most pernicious rationalization is that he has freely chosen to be what he is, for the illusion of choice precludes the struggle, the regret, which is necessary for spiritual survival:

> You loved me quite enough, it seems to-night.
> This must suffice me here. What would one have?
> In heaven, perhaps, new chances, one more chance—
> Four great walls in the New Jerusalem,
> Meted on each side by the angel's reed,
> For Leonard, Rafael, Agnolo and me
> To cover—the three first without a wife,

> While I have mine! So—still they overcome
> Because there's still Lucrezia,—as I choose.
> [B348]

That is, Andrea's contraction is premature and final. He *wills* his limits because he is afraid of *discovering* them.

Sludge and Bougram are not artists, but as hoaxers they are the next closest thing to poets. They share many of the concerns of the painters and are therefore worthy of brief consideration in this context. Blougram, who "believed, say, half he spoke" (B358), delivers an oration on the necessity of possibility, or the utility of contraction:

> You do despise me; your ideal of life
> Is not the bishop's; you would not be I.
> You would like better to be Goethe, now,
> Or Buonaparte, or, bless me, lower still,
> Count D'Orsay,—so you did what you preferred,
> Spoke as you thought, and, as you cannot help,
> Believed or disbelieved, no matter what,
> So long as on that point, whate'er it was,
> You loosed your mind, were whole and sole yourself.
> —That, my ideal never can include . . .
> . . . . . . . . . . . . . . . . . . . . . . . . . . . . . . . . . . . . . . . . . . . . .
> So, drawing comfortable breath again,
> You weigh and find, whatever more or less
> I boast of my ideal realized
> Is nothing in the balance when opposed
> To your ideal, your grand simple life,
> Of which you will not realize one jot.
> I am much, you are nothing; you would be all,
> I would be merely much: you beat me there.
> [B349-50]

In the end, Blougram is more flexible than Andrea, for though he insists on the necessity of choice, the little that is something, he does not fool himself into thinking that choice becomes necessity, that it is final:

> And now what are we? unbelievers both,
> Calm and complete, determinately fixed

To-day, to-morrow, and forever, pray?
You'll guarantee me that? Not so, I think!
In no wise! all we've gained is, that belief,
As unbelief before, shakes us by fits,
Confounds us like its predecessor. Where's
The gain? how can we guard our unbelief,
Make it bear fruit to us?—the problem here.
. . . . . . . . . . . . . . . . . . . . . . . . . . . . . . . . . .
All we have gained then by our unbelief
Is a life of doubt diversified by faith,
For one of faith diversified by doubt.
We called the chess-board white,—we call it black.

[B351]

Blougram knows what Gigadibs does not—that he is never as much at ease as he pretends to be. He does not exclude doubt as Gigadibs pretends to exclude certainty. We cannot fault the Bishop for rationalization because he is so conscious of his rationalization that if we wish to criticize him we must do so on the basis that the pretense of controlling rationalizations is itself a kind of rationalization— and Blougram seems to know this, too. Whatever our moral judgment of Blougram, we must admit that he is a born survivor. He walks "the giddy line midway" and refuses, unlike his interpreters, to be "classed and done with" (B353). Blougram's detractors implicitly admit that he is "right," faulting him only for being so *consciously* right.

The belief that "shakes us by fits" is the other side of the poet-hoaxer's sense of diminution, and it is evident even in the venial Sludge. Sludge, whose profession is conscious deception, is, after all, unable to convince himself that all his lies are lies:

This trade of mine—I don't know, can't be sure
But there was something in it, tricks and all!
. . . . . . . . . . . . . . . . . . . . . . . . . . . . . . . . . .
I don't know if I move your hand sometimes
When the spontaneous writing spreads so far,
If my knee lifts the table all that height,
Why the inkstand don't fall off the desk a-tilt,
Why the accordion plays a prettier waltz
Than I can pick out on the pianoforte,
Why I speak so much more than I intend,

56

Describe so many things I never saw.
I tell you, sir, in one sense, I believe
Nothing at all,—that everybody can,
Will, and does cheat: but in another sense
I'm ready to believe my very self—
That every cheat's inspired, and every lie
Quick with a germ of truth.

[B405, 410]

The diminished poet must back into truth and faith even as he backs into the quest. He must admit he can tell no truth, must both fear and confess the fatal irrelevance of the particular, the other, before it will speak for him. This is where hoax, whether gentle or grim, meets inspiration. In a poetry of divided awareness, of hoax, of deception and self-deception, concealment is the necessary concomitant of expression. The desire for the fatally irrelevant, for the insoluble, for the opaque, is the desire for the "fashioned" poem (as opposed to the "radiance" or "effluence" of the Shelleyan seer). The fashioned poem indeed protects the poet from exposure, but it also protects itself from dissolution, from transparency. This is the only type of poem that Browning and Hardy could feel. The synthetic faculty of one generation seems to create the analytical faculty of the next, and the Romantics in their poetry implied the knowledge, the critical mind, which, at least as the two Victorians saw it, made their innocence and their poetry impossible for later generations.

Necessity and possibility (habit and chaos, limitation and multiplicity, form and formlessness) are the rock and the whirlpool of Victorian poetry. Hardy flirts more dangerously with necessity and risks petrifaction. His poems, in speaking themselves, lift great weights, and their characteristic feature is heroic restraint. Browning skirts the maelstrom and becomes the prophet of possibility. The siren of one poet is the lifeline of the other—possibilities preserve the sentience of the monolithic Hardy, and necessity anchors the protean Browning.

Hardy's belief in his own diminution is not obvious, but he is willing to believe that no great writers were alive in his time: "A. J. B. ... dwelt with much emphasis on the decline of the literary art, and on his opinion that there were no writers of high rank living in these days. We hid our diminished heads ... What he said may have been true enough" (L253-54). This sentiment is by no means peculiar to Hardy or to his generation, but it is underlined in him by his sense of his hereditary social destiny: "The Dorset Hardys ... had the characteristics of an old family of spent social energies, that were revealed even in the Thomas Hardy of this memoir (as in his father and grandfather)" (L5). There is some question as to whether this observation was made by Florence Emily Hardy, the nominal author of the *Life*, or by Hardy himself, who seems to have written it, but we find the same sentiment in a quotation from Hardy's notebooks: "The decline and fall of the Hardys much in evidence hereabout ... So we go down, down, down" (L214-15). The most telling evidence for Hardy's sense of diminution, however, is in the poetry itself, in its willful refusal of vision:

> We are getting to the end of visioning
> The impossible within this universe,
> Such as that better whiles may follow worse,
> And that our race may mend by reasoning.
>
> We know that even as larks in cages sing
> Unthoughtful of deliverance from the curse
> That holds them lifelong in a latticed hearse,
> We ply spasmodically our pleasuring.
>
> And that when nations set them to lay waste
> Their neighbours' heritage by foot and horse,
> And hack their pleasant plains in festering seams,
> They may again,—not warely, or from taste,
> But tickled mad by some demonic force.—
> Yes. We are getting to the end of dreams!
> [CP886-87]

This self-denial is so strict and so persistent that Donald Davie sees it as an abdication:

> And so his poems, instead of transforming and displacing quantifiable reality or the reality of common sense, are on the contrary just so many glosses on that reality, which is conceived of as unchallengeably "given" and final. This is what makes it possible to say (once again) that he sold the

vocation short, tacitly surrendering the proudest claims traditionally made for the act of poetic imagination.[8]

There is some question as to whether Hardy's strategy is, or can be, successfully limiting, but this need not concern us until chapter four, when we shall examine the nature of Hardy's (largely involuntary) vision. What is important at this point is Hardy's unyielding decorum of diminution.

As his fashioning of Wessex suggests, Hardy is deliberately small and localized. Unlike Browning, he finds England in Italy, and once, having been reminded of a work called *The Queen of China*, he commented, "Oh yes, I remember. It is not a title that would naturally interest one."[9] Despite the laborious *Dynasts,* he is interested in large and unfamiliar events only insofar as they cross and mar individual lives, and he asserts that "there are certain questions which are made unimportant by their very magnitude" (L282). Browning is a historicist, and he finds as much texture and character in the mind of the Renaissance as he does in the slime of Caliban's swamp. Hardy lacks a great deal of this appetite for the indigestible, and he quickly wrests the familiar from the foreign. When he confronts the city in which Browning revels, his language cringes defensively and empties out:

> I busied myself to find a sure
>   Snug hermitage
> That should preserve my Love secure
>   From this world's rage;
> Where no unseemly saturnals,
>   Or strident traffic-roars,
> Or hum of intervolved cabals
>   Should echo at her doors.
>
> I laboured that the diurnal spin
>   of vanities
> Should not contrive to suck her in
>   By dark degrees,
> And cunningly operate to blur
>   Sweet teachings I had begun . . .
>                     [CP216]

Here, even the word "diurnal" is a distress signal. Wordsworth found its largeness felicitous:

A slumber did my spirit steal;
  I had no human fears:
She seemed a thing that could not feel
  The touch of earthly years.

No motion has she now, no force;
  She neither hears nor sees;
Rolled round in earth's diurnal course,
  With rocks, and stones, and trees.

For Hardy, however, its size and abstraction reek of mechanism, of the boredom he inevitably feels in the face of phenomena too vague and undifferentiated to be meaningful. We may recall "A Commonplace Day":

Nothing of tiniest worth
Have I wrought, pondered, planned; no one thing asking
                                    blame or praise,
  Since the pale corpse-like birth
Of this diurnal unit, bearing blanks in all its rays—
  Dullest of dull-hued Days!

[CP105]

In some of his best moments, Wordsworth moves from the fact of humanity to an intuition of a larger order. He can hear abstractions breathe, as in "She was a phantom of delight":

And now I see with eye serene
The very pulse of the *machine;*
A Being breathing thoughtful breath,
A Traveller between life and death . . . (emphasis mine)

In contrast, Hardy's "Amabel," which is bounced off this poem, discovers the danger, the mindlessness, in the "machine":

Her step's *mechanic* ways
Had lost the life of May's;
Her laugh, once sweet in swell,
  Spoilt Amabel.
      [CP6 emphasis mine]

Hardy is most comfortable looking through the other end of the telescope. He consistently substitutes the homely for the exotic, as in "Geographical Knowledge":

Where Blackmoor was, the road that led
  To Bath, she could not show,
Nor point the sky that overspread
  Towns ten miles off or so.

But that Calcutta stood this way,
  Cape Horn there figured fell,
That here was Boston, here Bombay,
  She could declare full well.

"My son's a sailor, and he knows
  All seas and many lands,
And when he's home he points and shows
  Each country where it stands.

"He's now just there—by Gib's high rock—
  And when he gets, you see,
To Portsmouth here, behind the clock,
  Then he'll come back to me!"

[CP270]

Blood is thicker than water, and human history pales before individual memory, as in "The Roman Road":

> no tall brass-helmed legionnaire
> Haunts it for me. Uprises there
> A mother's form upon my ken,
> Guiding my infant steps, as when
> We walked that ancient thoroughfare,
>       The Roman Road.
>           [CP248]

In "In Time of 'The Breaking of Nations'" the process of reduction, which is in the end a gentle form of irony, a deliberate act of forgetfulness, leads back into largeness, into the affirmation of a counter-transcendent:

> I
> Only a man harrowing clods
> In a slow silent walk
> With an old horse that stumbles and nods
> Half asleep as they stalk.

II
Only thin smoke without flame
  From the heaps of couch-grass;
Yet this will go onward the same
  Though Dynasties pass.

III
Yonder a maid and her wight
  Come whispering by:
War's annals will fade into night
  Ere their story die.

[CP511]

Hardy, through his willful division of human concerns, discovers Keats's nightingale in the generations of human lovers who are not allowed to remember "the weariness, the fever and the fret/ Here, where men sit and hear each other groan." Like Browning, he is menaced by the vagaries of abstraction, but he retreats not to the solidity of objects and characters but to the comforting familiarity of the archetypes he fingers as if they were smooth stones.

In the preface to *Wessex Poems*, Hardy warns that his "pieces are in large degree dramatic or personative in conception; and this even when they are not obviously so" (CP3), and he thought this admonition important enough to repeat verbatim upon the publication of *Poems of the Past and Present* (CP75). *Time's Laughingstocks* is preceded by his assertion that its poems are to be "regarded, in the main, as dramatic monologues by different characters" (CP175). In a sense, Hardy spoke more truly than he knew, for if it is a cliché that Browning's characters reveal Browning, Hardy, as we shall see in the chapter "Style and Self-Division," wrote about "other" people even when he thought he was writing about himself. In another sense, however, we tend to dismiss Hardy's remarks out of hand, for not all, or even many, of his poems pretend to be dramatic monologues, and those which do seem very far from what we have learned to expect from Browning or Shakespeare.

This is to judge Hardy's dramatic interests by irrelevant standards. He is not primarily concerned with rendering individuals or individual voices. His drama is self-drama, and it is not at all unfair to say that the *Collected Poems* contains few voices distinct from

the one we call Hardy's, and that those which strike us as different
are usually based on some poetic trick:

"O 'Melia, my dear, this does everything crown!
Who could have supposed I should meet you in Town?
And whence such fair garments, such prosperi-ty?"—
"O didn't you know I'd been ruined?" said she.

—"You left us in tatters, without shoes or socks,
Tired of digging potatoes, and spudding up docks;
And now you've gay bracelets and bright feathers three!"—
"Yes: that's how we dress when we're ruined," said she.

—"At home in the barton you said 'thee' and 'thou,'
And 'thik oon,' and 'theäs oon,' and 't'other'; but now
Your talking quite fits 'ee for high compa-ny!"—
"Some polish is gained with one's ruin," said she.

"Your hands were like paws then, your face blue and bleak,
But now I'm bewitched by your delicate cheek,
And your little gloves fit as on any la-dy!"—
"We never do work when we're ruined," said she.

"You used to call home-life a hag-ridden dream,
And you'd sigh and you'd sock; but at present you seem
To know not of megrims or melancho-ly!"—
"True. One's pretty lively when ruined," said she.

—"I wish I had feathers, a fine sweeping gown,
And a delicate face, and could strut about Town!"—
"My dear—a raw country girl, such as you be,
Cannot quite expect that. You ain't ruined," said she.

[CP145–46]

This is one of Hardy's most delightful poems, but we should not be
surprised that it is nearly unique. Here, character is defined
through extreme exaggeration, through the speed and lightness of
jog-trot, a rather limited poetic resource, and a large part of the
poem's charm derives from its consciousness of its own irrelevance.
Hardy does not encourage us to see the vast self-detachment of the
ruined maid as psychologically realistic, nor does he promulgate the
illusion that she and her smitten girlfriend are choosing their own
words. Similar observations can be made about the distinctive voice
of "Long-Plighted":

> Is it worth while, dear, now,
> To call for bells, and sally forth arrayed
> For marriage-rites—discussed, descried, delayed
>     So many years?
>
> Is it worth while, dear, now,
> To stir desire for old fond purposings,
> By feints that Time still serves for dallyings,
>     Though quittance nears?
>
> Is it worth while, dear, when
> The day being so far spent, so low the sun,
> The undone thing will soon be as the done,
>     And smiles as tears?
>
> Is it worth while, dear, when
> Our cheeks are worn, our early brown is gray;
> When, meet or part we, none says yea or nay,
>     Or heeds, or cares?
>
> Is it worth while, dear, since
> We still can climb old Yell'ham's wooded mounds
> Together, as each season steals its rounds
>     And disappears?
>
> Is it worth while, dear, since
> As mates in Mellstock churchyard we can lie,
> Till the last crash of all things low and high
>     Shall end the spheres?
>
>                                               [CP128]

This is also a fine poem, and its characterizing device, the use of the rising intonation of the interrogative to express timidity and tentativeness, is also of limited use for whole poems, though Hardy uses it sporadically with great success, and brilliantly in "Afterwards." Again, we are not encouraged to see the poem as much more than Hardy himself hovering over the plight of the aged lovers. There is no real attempt to individualize the speaker, and the *drama* of the poem is in its progression from the present to the end of the world, a progression so unmistakably Hardy's that it would be a blatant violation of dramatic decorum if there were any dramatic decorum to be violated. Hardy submits himself not to the character but to the single emotion arising from the situation, an emotion which belongs to him more than to his speaker:

> Hardy, in spite of a fascination with the grotesque which he shares with Browning, has no revelation of complexity in his speakers to compare with the Bishop who orders his tomb, Fra Lippo Lippi, Andrea del Sarto, Porphyria's lover, or the protagonists of "The Laboratory" and "My Last Duchess." In the form of the monologue favoured by Browning and Tennyson, the objective events and other characters concerned in the situation are filtered through the subjective screen of a speaker whose knowledge is limited by the presentness of his perspective.[10]

Hardy's diction and ideas are much too important and unvarying to be left to the discretion of characters. He is unable to postpone himself long enough to effect the "presentness," the independent presence, of which Jean Brooks speaks above. The long and short views in his poems assert themselves quickly and alternately. In "Heiress and Architect," the single voice and its presentness are brutally and repeatedly undercut by the voice that represents the distant perspective of "all things considered":

> "Shape me," she said, "high halls with tracery
> And open ogive-work, that scent and hue
> Of buds, and travelling bees, may come in through,
> The note of birds, and singings of the sea,
>     For these are much to me."
>
> "And idle whim!"
> Broke forth from him
> Whom nought could warm to gallantries:
> "Cede all these buds and birds, the zephyr's call,
> And scents, and hues, and things that falter all,
> And choose as best the close and surly wall,
>     For winters freeze."
>
> "Then frame," she cried, "wide fronts of crystal glass,
> That I may show my laughter and my light—
> Light like the sun's by day, the stars' by night—
> Till rival heart-queens, envying, wail, 'Alas,
>     Her glory!' as they pass."

"O maid misled!"
He sternly said
Whose facile foresight pierced her dire;
"Where shall abide the soul when, sick of glee,
It shrinks, and hides, and prays no eye may see?
Those house them best who house for secrecy,
    For you will tire."

"A little chamber, then, with swan and dove
Ranged thickly, and engrailed with rare device
Of reds and purples, for a Paradise
Wherein my love may greet me, I my Love,
    When he shall know thereof?"

"This, too, is ill,"
He answered still,
The man who swayed her like a shade.
"An hour will come when sight of such sweet nook
Would bring a bitterness too sharp to brook,
When brighter eyes have won away his look;
    For you will fade."

Then said she faintly: "O, contrive some way—
Some narrow winding turret, quite my own,
To reach a loft where I may grieve alone!
It is a slight thing; hence do not, I pray,
    This last dear fancy slay!"

"Such winding ways
Fit not your days,"
Said he, the man of measuring eye;
"I must even fashion as the rule declares,
To wit: Give space (since life ends unawares)
To hale a coffined corpse adown the stairs;
    For you will die."

                                        [CP67–68]

Although this poem, with its alternation of reasonably distinct
voices, is certainly dramatic, it is not a dramatic dialogue. The
speakers are neither real, nor consistent, nor dramatically inconsis-
tent. The architect recommends, in turn, secrecy and openness only
because Hardy's purpose is to thwart his romantic heiress, whose
purpose is solely to be at the mercy of the architect and his
inescapable verities. The poem, effective as it is, is merely a pseudo-

dramatic version of the contrasts of awareness which Hardy's poems normally accomplish in one voice:

> And the happy young housewife does not know
> That the woman beside her was first his choice,
> Till the fates ordained it could not be so. . . .
> Betraying nothing in look or voice
> The guest sits smiling and sips her tea,
> And he throws her a stray glance yearningly.
>
> [CP391]

This is not to denigrate "Heiress and Architect," which is a better poem than "At Tea," just quoted, but there is nothing indispensable in the division of its voices. Hardy's poems are most truly dramatic in that they are based on contrasts of awareness and that the omniscient perspective, whether stated or merely implied, does not erase the ignorant perspective but instead makes it tragic or poignant. The architect in Hardy speaks truly and often, but the feelings of the heiress remain necessary and real. As we have said, Hardy's poems, in their narrative presentation of ironies and incongruities, and in their lyric evocation of lost chances and other lives, depend upon a human ignorance which is for the poet a deliberate forgetfulness. Based as they are on contrasts of awareness, his poems are either obviously or implicitly broken in two:

> Briefly, Hardy's antinomial pattern works this way: thesis (usually a circumstance commonly accepted as good—marriage, youth, young love, the reunion of husband and wife) is set against antithesis (infidelity, age, death, separation) to form an ironic complex which is left unresolved. One might, generally speaking, say that the pattern is built on the relation of appearance and reality. In many of the poems this is true on a very simple level, as in "A Wife in London" or "Architectural Masks," which contrasts the exteriors of two houses with their occupants. But in more complicated poems the generalization is only valid if we recognize that appearance has its own kind of subjective truth—deluded love is still love—and is not merely an illusion to be or to put it another way, reality is not morally superior to appearance, though it is always more powerful and always destructive.[11]

Continuities are for Hardy, as for Browning, both transparent and impossible. He does not have the poetic confidence or the single-mindedness to say "I am learning," but the deep division of his poems says "I *have* learned." For Hardy, knowledge comes out of loss, and what man finds out is that he does not have what he thought he had, or that he once had something and did not know until it was gone, or that he does not want what he has, or simply that something is gone:

> She had learnt the lesson of renunciation, and was as familiar with the wreck of each day's wishes as with the diurnal setting of the sun. If her earthly career had taught her few book philosophies it had at least practised her in this. Yet her experience had consisted less in a series of pure disappointments than in a series of substitutions. Continually it had happened that what she had desired had not been granted her, and that what had been granted her she had not desired.[12]

The tragedy of life is the incongruity of desires and the means of fulfilling them, and Hardy conceives this incongruity in terms of a dissociation of knowledge (or power) and love, a dissociation which is also, profoundly, Browning's, and which corresponds exactly to the dual perspective of Hardy's poetry. In this connection, Hardy's troubling and nakedly abstract parables of the gods are relevant, for they are the most direct statements of this paradox. Hardy creates the gods in his own image. In "Doom and She," as in Hardy's vision of human existence, love and knowledge, ends and means, are irreconcilable:

I

There dwells a mighty pair
Slow, statuesque, intense—
Amid the vague Immense:
None can their chronicle declare,
Nor why they be, nor whence.

II

Mother of all things made,
Matchless in artistry,
Unlit with sight is she.—
And though her ever well-obeyed
Vacant of feeling he.

III
The Matron mildly asks—
A throb in every word—
"Our clay-made creatures, lord,
How fare they in their mortal tasks
Upon Earth's bounded bord?

IV
"The fate of those I bear,
Dear lord, pray turn and view,
And notify me true;
Shapings that eyelessly I dare
Maybe I would undo.

VI
"World-weaver!" he replies,
"I scan all thy domain;
But since nor joy nor pain
It lies in me to recognize,
Thy questionings are vain.

[CP 108-9]

At other times, there is only one god, the god of power, and the poet takes the part of love:

I saw him steal the light away
  That haunted in her eye:
It went so gently none could say
More than that it was there one day
  And missing by-and-by.

I asked: "Why do you serve her so?
  Do you, for some glad day,
Hoard these her sweets—?" He said, "O no,
They charm not me; I bid Time throw
  Them carelessly away."

Said I: "We call that cruelty—
  We, your poor mortal kind."
He mused. "The thought is new to me.
Forsooth, though I men's master be.
  Theirs is the teaching mind!"

[CP261-62]

In a universe ruled by unconscious powers, consciousness is a disease, what Hardy calls, "the disease of feeling" (CP260), and he sometimes yearns for its cure—"Ere nescience shall be reaffirmed/ How long, how long?" (CP260). In the past it has been fashionable to accuse nineteenth-century poets such as Tennyson of escapism, of seeking the land of the lotus. This is part of the legendary dissociation of sensibility. The criticism is, in a sense, valid, but it is not a criticism and it is only half valid. Hardy's (and Browning's) investigations of the anti-idyll, the subordination of feeling to knowledge, make it clear that the ironic mode is also a kind of escapism or forgetfulness. The "nescience" of Hardy's cosmic power is the invulnerability of the ironic or knowing perspective in his poetry. While the perspective of unawareness in Hardy's poetry involves the bliss of ignorance, happiness based on the exclusion of knowledge, the ironic perspective offers a painlessness achieved through the exclusion of love. For Browning and Hardy, both irony and pity, knowledge and love, are the result of instinctive and successive contractions of consciousness. Their sensibilities may well be dissociated, but they are not one-sided; nor, with its alternate longings for death and calls to duty, is Tennyson's. Hardy and Browning stay conscious by vacillating between two states of unconsciousness. The alternation of exclusions in Browning's monologues is subtle and constant, and we perceive them as belonging to the character, or as changes in our judgment of the character. Hardy's smaller and subtler alternations (in diction, for example) are also perceived as character, but as the *poet's* character, and they are partially overshadowed by the more obvious bifurcations of his poems. These larger and smaller divisions may be described as the succession of repression and return, or of exclusion and inclusion, or simply as an exchange of exclusions. Hardy's poetry, accordingly, depends on what Samuel Hynes calls "reticence as a mode of expression."[13]

A sense of the inevitability of this alternation is necessary to an understanding of Hardy's integration of particulars, especially natural details, in his poetry. Hardy's observations often fall upon us in great chunks only to be dismissed as irrelevant and inexplicable.

Their function is at first unclear:

> The rain smites more and more,
> The east wind snarls and sneezes;
> Through the joints of the quivering door
>   The water wheezes.
>
> The tip of each ivy-shoot
> Writhes on its neighbour's face;
> There is some hid dread afoot
>   That we cannot trace.
>
> Is it the spirit astray
> Of the man at the house below
> Whose coffin they took in to-day?
>   We do not know.

[CP438]

There is nothing at all objectionable about this poem—it is very effective—but it is nevertheless true that it changes direction, in a fashion typical of Hardy, and without any apparent reason, after the sixth line. If the second half of the poem were lost, it could be replaced with any number of Hardyesque anecdotes. There is no necessary relationship between the weather and the speaker's meditation. There is, of course, a vague connection between the aggressive landscape and the poet's uneasiness, but there is no vision of their inevitable equivalence. As Samuel Hynes says,

> "This is a very characteristic poem in that all we are allowed to *know* is the substantive situation—the wind, the rain, and the writhing ivy. The dread is in what we do not and cannot know, the forces or the emptiness behind the actual. The poem does not explain anything, nor does it set this particular experience in the context of any system of belief; rather it dramatizes man's *inability* to explain, his ignorance and his horror.[14]

All we can say at this point is that this particular natural description is somehow ominous, that it partakes of a purposeful purposelessness. In more extreme examples, the only connection between the

observer and the elaborate landscape is one of noticing or not
noticing:

> Orion swung southward aslant
> Where the starved Egdon pine-trees had thinned,
> The Pleiads aloft seemed to pant
> With the heather that twitched in the wind;
> But he looked on indifferent to sights such as these,
> Unswayed by love, friendship, home joy or home sorrow,
> And wondered to what he would march on the morrow.
>
> [CP512]

Though such descriptive passages are often, if not here, exquisite,
and though their absence might destroy the poems which contain
them, the reader is justified in feeling a kind of impatience, for that
impatience is dictated by the poet. The impatience, the sense of
delay, the ominousness, is the result of the fact that these passages
are repressions or exclusions of the human meaning which is
approaching us (and which often creeps into the images themselves).
The repression is partly deliberate and partly unconscious. That is,
Hardy's poems often come to him as scenes, as natural images, and
grow conscious of themselves as they proceed. Hardy frequently
seems aware of this process:

> The broad, bald moon edged up where the sea was wide,
>   Mild, mellow-faced;
> Beneath, a tumbling twinkle of shines, like dyed,
>   A trackway traced
> To the shore, as of petals fallen from a rose to waste,
>   In its overblow,
> And fluttering afloat on inward heaves of the tide: —
> All this so plain; yet the rest I did not know.
>
> [CP678]

That is, the apparently detachable particulars are in fact a manifesta-
tion of a concealed dynamic. The *accumulation* of natural details in
Hardy's mind is accompanied, paradoxically, by a growing sense of
incompleteness, a sense of the absence or repression of the human
emotions which will eventually give direction to the poem. This
process might be decribed by as bland a phrase as "setting the
scene," but it is in fact an organized and ominous exclusion which
opens up the poem even as it fails:

Inside a window, open, with undrawn blind,
  There plays and sings
A lady unseen a melody undefined:
  And where the moon flings
Its shimmer a vessel crosses, whereon to the strings
  Plucked sweetly and low
Of a harp they dance. Yea, such did I mark. That, behind,
My Fate's masked face crept near me I did not know!

[CP678]

Detail is significant for what it is, but it is ominous for what it is not. When Hardy insists that it has "nothing to do" with him—

A car comes up, with lamps full-glare,
  That flash upon a tree:
  It has nothing to do with me,
And whangs along in a world of its own,
  Leaving a blacker air;
And mute by the gate I stand again alone,
  And nobody pulls up there.

[CP705]

it has, in fact, created him, for he characteristically discovers himself through his absence. He defines himself through the very irrelevance of the particular, and his concentration on the other crystallizes his feeling of isolation. Hardy's deliberately anti-Wordsworthian landscapes are products of this process. In "The Darkling Thrush," (discussed in chapter one), nature is manipulated and narrowed until it is ominous, until it can no longer contain the self, until the poem recoils, "At once a song arose among/The bleak twigs overhead," and the self is expelled, defining itself through its escape, through its new sense of what it is not: "some blessed hope whereof he knew/And I was unaware."

  This movement is normally invisible. It precedes poems or is broken up and buried inside them, and it is only when Hardy chooses to commit his struggle, his initial confrontation with nothingness, to the page that we are permitted to see the workings of his mind. Hardy left relatively few poems with so telling a separation of detail and self (more of which will be examined in the next chapter), but the opposing forces of omen and delay can readily be seen to be central to a poetry of divided awareness. The persistence of any one

73

perspective signals with increasing urgency the necessity for its complement. In this lies a possible explanation for the elaborate stanzaic slowness of narrative poems that are apparently concerned only with the efficient relation of a story. The slowness tries to forget the inevitable, but its very persistence becomes ominous and forces us to remember.

As we shall see, the large terms "omen" and "delay" are the macrocosm of a microcosm which involves the minute workings of diction, form, and rhythm, for Hardy often divides himself on this smaller scale by choosing words which leap from their context, in stretching from words which are his to words which reject him, and in the contractions and expansions of his lines. These, along with his handling of detail, bespeak the ubiquitous but quiet oppositions of necessity and possibility. Hardy is unable to commit himself permanently. He wants both ignorance and knowledge, both delay and speed, and he is threatened by the limitation and incompleteness of the perspectives he adopts. He devotes himself to a perspective only as long as he can stand its claustrophobia. Then he withdraws until the vertigo of the all forces new involvement and new contraction.

# 3
# STYLE AND
# SELF-DIVISION

*Jude the Obscure*, published in 1895, had alienated much of the literary establishment, and Hardy, whose distrust of critics verged on paranoia, was prepared for a further beating when, later in the same decade, he committed his poetry to the presses. By the time of the appearance of *Wessex Poems* (1898) and *Poems of the Past and Present* (1901), however, Hardy's notorious atheism, pessimism, and moral outrageousness were relatively dead issues for the reviewers, and his ventures in poetry were found objectionable less for their characteristically grim vision than for their difficult idiosyncrasies of style. As Hardy grudgingly admits in the *Life,* the reception of his poetry was not unreasonably hostile: "the poems were reviewed in the customary periodicals—mostly in a friendly tone, even in a tone of respect, and with praise for many pieces in the volume; though by some critics not without umbrage at Hardy's having taken the liberty to adopt another vehicle of expression than prose fiction without consulting them" (L299).

Still, his readers were baffled and repelled by his poetic manner, and they did not hesitate to say so. One anonymous reviewer was horrified by the "slovenly, slipshod, uncouth verses, stilted in sentiment, poorly conceived and worse wrought,"[1] and another complains of Hardy's "lack of metrical finish" and his "technical inexpertness" and finds his "strong, grim hand . . . too heavy for poetry."[2] Even E. K. Chambers, who had significant praise for Hardy's intentions—"There is no finish or artifice about it: the note struck is strenuous, austere, forcible; it is writing that should help to give backbone to a literature which certainly errs on the side of flabbiness. And this applies to diction as well as sentiment"—objected to "woodenness of rhythm and a needlessly inflated diction."[3] The puzzlement of the critics is understandable, for Hardy himself was not completely aware of what he was doing, and his counterattack in the *Life* is rather naive:

> That the author loved the art of concealing art was undiscerned. For instance, as to rhythm. Years earlier he had decided that too regular a beat was bad art. He had fortified himself in his opinion by thinking of the analogy of architecture, between which art and that of poetry he had discovered, to use his own words, that there existed a close and curious parallel, both arts, unlike some others, having to carry a rational content inside their artistic form. He knew that in architecture cunning irregularity is of enormous worth, and it is obvious that he carried on into his verse, perhaps in part unconsciously, the Gothic art-principle in which he had been trained—the principle of spontaneity, found in mouldings, tracery, and such like—resulting in the 'unforeseen' (as it has been called) character of his metres and stanzas, that of stress rather than of syllable, poetic texture rather than poetic veneer; the latter kind of thing, under the name of 'constructed ornament,' being what he, in common with every Gothic student, had been taught to avoid as the plague. He shaped his poetry accordingly, introducing metrical pauses, and reversed beats; and found for his trouble that some particular line of a poem exemplifying this principle was greeted with a would-be jocular remark that such a line 'did not make for immortality' (L300–301).

Hardy responds as if the whole misunderstanding could be attributed to an occasional reversed beat, as if he himself had discovered the utility of metrical irregularity and the fact that lines can be founded on an accentual rather than a syllabic basis, and as if he were an apostle of a new gothicism—a faded critical category which had been trundled onstage since the eighteenth century to defend the likes of Spenser and Shakespeare. This is all slightly embarrassing, but if we can allow the confusion of Hardy's critics, we can surely understand the innocence of the self-educated Hardy, for no less a personage than the vastly literate Coleridge had shamed himself even more explicitly by announcing, in the preface to *Christabel,* his own discovery of the accentual line.

It seems to be the fate of new poets to misunderstand their places in the history of style and to misinterpret the rules under which their predecessors operated. Perhaps this is just as well, for each generation of writers manages to be new in ways that the counting of accents and syllables cannot describe, anymore than it can account for the variations among individual human voices. All this is not to say that we, even with the advantage of hindsight, are able to explain the particular effects of Hardy's poetry much more readily than he or his contemporaries. Although there is a growing consensus as to which poems comprise the Hardy canon, the chances are that any convention of Hardy amateurs required to assess the details of the best poems would soon come to blows, or to silence, over which of their various oddities of rhythm, diction, and form are fresh and saving and which are awkward and merely odd. Indeed, the one inescapable characteristic of Hardy's poetry is that it continually devours its own context, that it backs away from itself through constant changes of perspective. Hardy's uneasy decorum may foster the curious critical attitude that Davie deplores: "Affection for Hardy the poet is general, and quite often (in Britain, at any rate) it is fervent; but it is ruinously shot through with protectiveness, even condescension."[4] Davie himself is scarcely protective, but he is occasionally condescending, and if we must nevertheless rank him as one of Hardy's very best readers, it is because Hardy's poetry, with its tentative contexts and interrupted perspectives, invites condescension, in the neutral sense of the word. Hardy seldom writes with the authority of Yeats, or even Browning. He does not manhandle his reader, but instead asks him (politely) to excuse the potentially inexcusable, to tolerate or to ignore entirely whatever seems too jagged or wayward.

Many critics have commented on the difficulty of selecting Hardy's poetry, and it is surely true that the strongest and weakest poems are blasted from the same rock. Once we have decided that Hardy is wonderful or intolerable, it is easy to dismiss the fresh with the awkward or to allow the worst to masquerade with the best. Hardy depends so heavily on our condescension that we are often expected to carry his personal associations into poems where they are not independently established. We are encouraged to prop up a weak stanza with the memory of a better version in another poem, to construct the best of all possible Hardy poems using the fragments of other poems, which, judged as wholes, range from mediocre to stunning. Selection is often necessary, but for the potentially sympathetic reader, it is not the best way to meet Hardy, who grows on his readers but seldom takes them by storm.

The stylistic (as well as the thematic) "message" of Hardy's poetry is that we are incapable of responding to, and in, necessity's vistas of sameness. Tyrannical order is as incomprehensible as chaos. The small irregularities and oddities of Hardy's poems, like the deep divisions, signal change, but they are excursions which, in the end, have little to do with freedom, for they are part of a round-trip whose purpose is the rediscovery and refeeling of the familiar. Though the poet cannot escape necessity, he must remain aware at every point that he is struggling with it, and almost all of Hardy's stylistic peculiarities can be traced back to his need for *effort* in poetry, his sense of the difficulty of true feeling. Accordingly, negative criticism of the poetry is of two kinds. One is repelled by the laboriousness of much of the verse, and finds it "stilted," "wooden," "heavy," etc., and another finds that, despite all the effort, feeling is too easily achieved, as when we say that some of Hardy's ironies can be gratuitous or that his sentimentalism is occasionally mawkish. Both kinds of criticism can be valid, for though Hardy's oddities are always explicable in terms of *his* needs, they are not always justifiable in terms of *ours*.

For Browning and Hardy, language is a highly volatile substance which vaporizes without constant stretching, cramping, and roughing up. They must feel, in the tactile as well as the emotional sense, their lines; and their habits of syntax, meter, diction, and line formation bespeak an obsession with shape. In the terms of the essay on Shelley, they produce "works" rather than "effluences," and the work involved in creation is communicated to the reader. Their poems are artifacts—they assert their madeness, their physicality. Hardy, unlike Browning, "rarely used images involving the 'contact' senses of touch and taste,"[5] and this, along with his abhorrence of physical intimacy makes the *intellectual* tactility of his poetry all the more striking and significant.[6] Hardy's contortions are primarily matters of diction, pacing, perspective, meter, and form, and they can be differentiated from Browning's, which extend to syntax and imagery, and which J. Hillis Miller explains in terms of a passion for the "inmost center of things":

> Browning wants to make the movement, sound, and texture of his verse an imitation of the vital matter of its subject, whether that subject is animate or inanimate, molten lava, flower, bird, beast, fish, or man. He thinks of matter, in whatever form, as something dense, heavy, rough, and strong-flavored, and there is for him a basic similarity between all forms of life—they are all strong solid substance inhabited by a vital energy. There are everywhere two things: the thick weight of matter, and within it an imprisoned vitality which seethes irresistibly out. The particular forms, however finely developed, are still rooted in the primal mud, and the means of expressing one are not unrelated to the means of expressing the other. It is by imitation of the roughness of a thing that one has most chance to get inside of it. Things are not made of smooth appearances, but of the dense inner core which is best approached through heavy language.[7]

If the only force active in Browning's personality were a desire for otherness, his poetry would surely be even more clotted and thingly than it is, and this passage would have no relevance for Hardy, who is noticeably less interested in the textures of objects and characters; but Miller describes only the adventure with the whirlpool, only the colonizing tendency of poetry. Even here it is only half of the truth, for pure thingliness is fatal, and Browning's fragmentary crystallizations are shored against a variety of ruin. But the rock, too, has its attractions, and the style of Browning and Hardy defends against the consequences of its takeover—the unfeeling sameness, the vagueness, which cannot, at least not without danger, be embraced. Hardy is the clarion of the rock, and his thirst for shape is less a desire to inhabit the other (though it is this) than an escape from the gravity of vagueness, a need to create an insoluble and independent, if momentary, shape. In the end, even this is an oversimplification, for he often finds himself in rebellion against straitjackets of his own fabrication, but the first generalization which must be made about Hardy is, nevertheless, that he can only live in small rooms he builds by himself.

Accordingly, Hardy is first and last a stanzaic poet, and is most comfortable within the varying yet rocklike limits of his self-imposed and sometimes mechanical forms. He seems to associate blank verse with a kind of greatness or expansiveness which is normally alien to his interests, and it is virtually absent from the *Collected Poems*. The vaporousness of the unrhymed portions of *The Dynasts* and *The Queen of Cornwall* attests to the wisdom of this instinct. Hardy could not follow Shakespeare successfully, Milton was entirely out of the question, and Romantic blank verse is propelled by an imposing single-mindedness which usually embarrassed him. Blank verse makes demands on the reader's capacity for interest and excitement that the modest and diminished Hardy seldom has the confidence to make. Although he is far more successful with the couplet, it is not one of his favorite forms:

> Strange it is this speechless thing,
> Subject to our mastering,
> Subject for his life and food
> To our gift, and time, and mood
> Timid pensioner of us Powers,
> His existence ruled by ours,
> Should—by crossing at a breath
> Into safe and shielded death,
> By the merely taking hence
> Of his insignificance—
> Loom as largened to the sense,
> Shape as part, above man's will,
> Of the Imperturbable.

As a prisoner, flight debarred,
Exercising in a yard,
Still retain I, troubled, shaken,
Mean estate, by him forsaken;
And this home, which scarcely took
Impress from his little look,
By his faring to the Dim
Grows all eloquent of him.

[CP622]

This excerpt contains some truly excellent writing, though one could wish it were not about a cat, but its most striking feature is its anonymity—it does not sound at all like Hardy (and "excellent writing" is not the kind of phrase we use about Hardy even when he is more than excellent). Its movement and authority are positively Yeatsian, and one wonders if some nearly imperceptible undertow of mock-heroism allowed Hardy to write in such a broad and assured manner.

Browning, at once more self-assertive and self-denying, does nearly all of his best work in blank verse and couplets, but only because his special instincts permit him to shape and cramp them in ways that the more deliberate Hardy could not. Browning's blank verse leans backward in such a way as to emphasize the line breaks even as he storms through them, and he actually creates a subliminal expectation of rhyme. Then, too, his syntax is so crabbed and twisted that each sentence carves a stanza out of the verse paragraph:

Do you see this Ring?
'Tis Rome-work, made to match
(By Castellani's imitative craft)
Etrurian circlets found, some happy morn,
After a dropping April; found alive
Spark-like 'mid unearthed slope-side figtree-roots
That roof old Tombs at Chiusi: soft, you see,
Yet crisp as jewel-cutting. There's one trick,
(Craftsmen instruct me) one approved device
And but one, fits such slivers of pure gold
As this was,—such mere oozings from the mine,

Virgin as oval tawny pendent tear
At beehive-edge when ripened combs o'erflow,—
To bear the file's tooth and the hammer's tap ...

[B414]

Here, parentheses, dashes, interjections, unexpected caesuras, and precipitous line breaks create rapid changes of pressure within the line. The result is a paradoxical blend of speed and deliberateness. Browning's mind veers wildly in all directions, but the rhythm and syntax are so uncertain that, like a dancer off balance, we come down harder on the stresses when we finally determine them. In this way, Browning uses speech rhythms to shape the lines internally, and he performs similar operations of couplets:

That's my last Duchess painted on the wall,
Looking is if she were alive. I call
That piece a wonder, now; Frà Pandolf's hands
Worked busily a day and there she stands.
Will 't please you sit and look at her? I said
"Frà Pandolf" by design, for never read
Strangers like you that pictured countenance,
The depth and passion of its earnest glance,
But to myself they turned ...

[B252]

The late caesuras in lines 2 and 5 of this excerpt are characteristic of Browning's stretching and cramping technique. That is, "Will 't please you sit and look at her" goes gasping along to a period, while "I said" is squeezed against the wall at the end of the line. This all contributes to the sense of terrible control which Browning reserves for his most deliberate, evasive, and eloquent speakers. Browning's mind is extremely parenthetical—

At the meal we sit together:
  *Salve tibi!* I must hear
Wise talk of the kind of weather,
  Sort of season, time of year:
*Not a plenteous cork-crop: scarcely*
  *Dare we hope oak-galls, I doubt:*
*What's the Latin name for "parsley"?*
  What's the Greek name for Swine's Snout?

[B167]

and its relentless qualifications, its disconnections, verge on the technique of collage, which, as art critics tell us, emphasizes the materials of art. In the end, Browning's apparent shapelessness implies a more primitive and vital kind of shape.

Hardy is neither so quick nor so slow, and his unit of rhythm is seldom less than a full line and seldom more. He stays in touch with himself and his poems through an exaggeration of the successive constrictions and relaxations of his stanzas, through the tensions and releases of rhyme, rhythm, and variable line length. Although this is most obvious in his most shapely and intricate stanzas, it is also apparent in simple forms such as that of "Without Ceremony":

> It was your way, my dear,
> To vanish without a word
> When callers, friends, or kin
> Had left, and I hastened in
> To rejoin you, as I inferred.
>
> And when you'd a mind to career
> Off anywhere—say to town—
> You were all on a sudden gone
> Before I had thought thereon,
> Or noticed your trunks were down.
>
> So, now that you disappear
> For ever in that swift style,
> Your meaning seems to me
> Just as it used to be:
> "Good-bye is not worth while!"
> [CP323]

The first three lines of each stanza are relatively swift and loose, and no rhyme impedes their flow. It is characteristic of Hardy that the fourth lines, the first to rhyme, should somehow be more difficult. Treating the normally easy couplet rhyme not as a goal but as a wall, they bog down as if to avoid hitting it at great speed. They struggle against expectation, and the result is a constriction of the middle of the stanza which Hardy could easily have avoided had he not felt the need for an anchor, a new perspective, to keep the poem from evaporating into the breezy speed which his lesser contemporaries called "polish," but which he apprehended as lack of feeling. Feeling requires effort, and effort is expressed through a change of pace wrought by the thwarting of expectation.

For the unalterably elegiac Hardy, last lines, whether of individual stanzas or of entire poems, are absolutely crucial, for he must decide between release and repression of emotion. Lastness in itself is a very important concept for Hardy, and he communicates this to his readers—we often find ourselves lending weight to entirely trivial last lines merely because we have become used to weight, to sadness, at that point, and even the most neutral stanzas become vaguely elegiac. At any rate, the final lines of these stanzas exhibit the widest variation in purpose, and what they show is Hardy postponing a complete release of emotion until the end of the poem. He could easily have smoothed out "To rejoin you, as I inferred" by the omission of "as" and the elimination of the jammed accents of "rejoin you," but he uses the slowness, the difficulty, to express the tentativeness, and ultimately the error, of the speaker's inference. The total effect is one of restraint or repression. In contrast, the final line of the second stanza is relatively easy, but complete release of emotions is thwarted by the tight consonance of the town-gone-thereon-down endings and the indirectness of "Or noticed your trunks were down." This tightness seems to necessitate the opening "So" of the third stanza. "So" is a conjunction Hardy uses when, as in "Transformations" (where the four end words are also similar in sound), the sound of a poem has resolved itself before the emotion or sense has been worked out:

> These grasses must be made
> Of her who often prayed,
> Last century, for repose;
> And the fair girl long ago
> Whom I often tried to know
> May be entering this rose.
>
> So, they are not underground . . .
> [CP443]

In both poems, the lines are individually apprehended, and they tend to be isolated even when they are enjambed. Hardy, in fact, uses whole lines the way most poets use metrical feet—as regularities or irregularities—and makes them conscious of the boxlike limits within which they must function. They are cramped into, or stretched over, a frame, and they seem hewn rather than effused.

These effects are even more pronounced when Hardy uses alternate rhyme in conjunction with lines of varying length:

> You lacked the eye to understand
> Those friends offhand
> Whose mode was crude, though whose dim purport
> Outpriced the courtesies of the bland.
>
> I am now the only being who
> Remembers you
> It may be. What a waste that Nature
> Grudged soul so dear the art its due!
>
> [CP408]

In Hardy's hands, this kind of pattern becomes one of continuous reconsideration, of speeding and slowing, of approach and withdrawal. The dropping off which accompanies the shift to a short line is heard almost as a parenthesis, as a retreat from an established level of discourse, and the shift back to the long line is a laborious summoning of powers. The built-in uncertainty of the length of the lines further isolates them, despite their grammatical relationships. This is the kind of shaping Hardy substitutes for Browning's rapid argumentative leaps, and he enjoys the effect so much that he often counterfeits it by indenting every other line in stanzas composed of lines of equal lengths. Through variations in line length, Hardy can wrest even the inimical couplet to his purposes:

> You did not walk with me
> Of late to the hill-top tree
> By the gated ways,
> As in earlier days;
> You were weak and lame.
> So you never came,
> And I went alone, and I did not mind,
> Not thinking of you as left behind.
>
> I walked up there to-day
> Just in the former way;
> Surveyed around
> The familiar ground

> By myself again:
> What difference, then?
> Only that underlying sense
> Of the look of a room on returning thence.
>
> [CP320]

Hardy's freedom in the matter of line length is actually another of his self-imposed limitations, for it is only when the size of a line is subject to variation that it becomes significant in itself. Consequently, this habit is finally a source not of relaxation but of increased tension:

> It was when
> Whirls of thick waters laved me
> Again and again,
> That something arose and saved me:
> Yea, it was then.
>
> [CP491]

Although the effect is nearly imperceptible, the ear (or the eye, or whatever reads for us) tends to equalize the lines by trying to read the long ones more quickly and the short ones more slowly, and Hardy encourages this endeavor by making the rhythm of the short lines tighter and/or more difficult to determine. By taking freedoms with the lengths of the lines, Hardy introduces another and almost subliminal principle of order and tension which is closely related to quantity. The principle, like all of Hardy's principles, is most in force when it is being violated, when Hardy makes the swift reading of the longer lines, especially when they are also last lines, impossible, as in the first stanza of ''In Front of the Landscape,'' quoted above, or in:

> I mark the months in liveries dank and dry,
> The noontides many-shaped and hued;
> I see the nightfall shades subtrude,
> And hear the monotonous hours clang negligently by.
>
> [CP43]

In these cases, the emotional effect is dissipation without release, and Hardy often associates it with ''custom'' or ''monotony,'' with time moving too slowly, with boredom or frustration. It is not surprising that a man whose thoughts and feelings are so dominated by time would need to incorporate a sense of timing into his style, but for Hardy the varying speeds of rhymed and unrhymed lines and of lines of different lengths and difficulties are almost more important than the visibility or invisibility of the metrical pattern. Indeed, metrical expectation is often primarily the means to control pace. In a poetry of heroic restraint, feeling and difficulty are closely allied, and each degree of difficulty, each pace, corresponds to a mood or a perspective. Many of Hardy's lines are formed under such tremendous metrical pressures that the pattern, though not the expectation of a pattern, disappears. Jean Brooks says of the last line of the following stanza, for example, that it cannot be spoken "without placing a major stress on each word":[8]

> A time there was—as one may guess
> And as, indeed, earth's testimonies tell—
> Before the birth of consciousness,
> When all went well.
>
> [CP260]

Brooks is undoubtedly correct. Had Hardy written "when all was well," the line could more easily have been interpreted as iambic (whĕn aĺl wăs wéll), but for whatever reason, "went" (probably because it ends with a harder sound) demands a stronger stress than "was," and this stress *retroactively* changes the stress on "when," for it is impossible, in this case, to read "whĕn aĺl wént wéll." This retroactive qualification, or rather its frequency in Hardy's verse, is further evidence that Hardy's unit of rhythm is the line, for it is very often impossible to determine stresses in the beginning of lines without taking into account those at the end. This retroactivity, along with the varying speeds of the lines, points to Hardy's small-scale self-divisions and the attendant workings of omen and delay. It is part of the necessary effort of his poetry. Brooks says that "the reader's uncertainties on the placing of stress may be art rather than incompetence—a required contribution to the sense of the difficulties of emergent human consciousness struggling with the intractable denseness of matter,"[9] and in so saying she outlines Hardy's defiance of, and compliance with, gravity, the battle with necessity which he wages in order to feel.

Though four consecutive stresses is the extreme of Hardy's technique, it is by no means uncommon, especially in his most visionary moments. Ransom says of "Channel Firing" that its "finest technical detail" is the "forced stresses which the meter places upon the last syllables of the final words: starlít Stone-hénge,"[10] and one could easily read four consecutive stresses into the last lines of the first two stanzas of "During Wind and Rain":

> They sing their dearest songs—
> He, she, all of them—yea,
> Treble and tenor and bass,
>     And one to play;
> With the candles mooning each face....
>     Ah, no; the years O!
> How the sick leaves reel down in throngs!
>
> They clear the creeping moss—
> Elders and juniors—aye,
> Making the pathways neat
>     And the garden gay;
> And they build a shady seat....
>     Ah, no; the years, the years;
> See, the white storm-birds wing across!
>                         [CP465–66]

"How the sick leaves reel down in throngs" defeats normal scansion, though its tensions would not exist without the *expectation* of a pattern. In the end, words become not stressed or unstressed syllables but units of time. Their enunciation is noticeably slowed as we unconsciously insert unstressed silences, pauses, between the words —they become notes, and the line almost demands to be sung, as do also "He, she, all of them—aye" and "Ah, no; the years, O!" This, and not the easy lilt of regular iambic, is what Hardy meant when he called his poems songs. "During Wind and Rain" is perhaps the most radical example of Hardy's equation of pace and perspective, his profound accommodation of style to the paradoxes of necessity and possibility, but it is also one of his very finest poems. It clearly embodies his characteristic opposition of "now" (or "then") and "all things considered" on the thematic level, but in addition, the lines are so isolated by their differences in pace and difficulty that each seems to function as an approach or an avoidance, an omen or a delay.

That we can perceive Hardy's minute changes in perspective and speed as ominous or dilatory implies that we have been led to expect to be taken somewhere. Indeed, part of Hardy is always ahead of himself, brooding on the end and forcing retroactive qualifications. The other part is in the process of rejoining it (by the long way) in a simple truth which has momentarily been excluded, forgotten, or, as Hardy would have said, "un-known." Whatever Hardy says is the first clause of a sentence which continues with "but" and closes somewhere in the dimension of loss. This is partly a matter of storytelling, and it accounts in part for the unbearable deliberateness of some of the narrative poems, but it also functions on a level which is virtually independent of content and theme—it is the rhythm of his feelings. The expansions and contractions, variations in speed and difficulty, changes in distance, are shuffled and reshuffled until reticence is expression and delay is omen.

If this theorizing is somewhat vague, its application is not. Everyone agrees that Hardy is a "rough poet," but Hynes's attempt to equate roughness with freedom is misguided, as when he says:

> Hardy's thought, while it had not achieved a system of belief, had freed him from traditional belief, and with this philosophical freedom went a poetical freedom as great, and as empty. Chance rules Hardy's universe, and often it seems to determine his style as well. And why, after all, in a lawless universe should there be laws governing poetry? Why *not* make poems out of clashing incongruities, since this is the way the world is?[11]

Hardy's poems are written at the moment when conventions are *strongest*, the moment when it is clear both that they are "merely" habits and that mere habit rules the universe. As we have seen, only the absolute primacy of metrical expectation can create Hardy's jaggedness, his illusion of freedom. There are no variations without something to vary. Whitman and late Lawrence are free poets, but they are not rough, no matter how clotted, in that they are not retroactive. If Hardy's verse could be read as prose, it would be free, but it cannot be. The very oddness of his idiosyncrasies proclaims the gravity, the tyranny, of form and decorum, of habit and necessity. Hardy cannot discard conventions. Instead, he polarizes himself into obedience and rebellion. Each is only a temporary escape from, or un-knowing of, the other, and they are constantly exchanging identities.

Similar generalizations can be made with respect to Hardy's repertoire of stanzas, of which Hynes says,

> They are not, in most cases, particularly appropriate to their subjects, and certainly Gosse's implication that Hardy was consistently capable of organic forms is quite inaccurate. It should be apparent (and one is surprised that it wasn't apparent to Hardy) that elaborate, irregular stanzas could not be appropriate for poems which have a strong dramatic or narrative aspect.[12]

One must agree that Hardy's choice of forms is arbitrary, though his *use* of the forms he chooses is always characteristic. This, again, is not the same as saying, with Hynes, that Hardy is "anti-formalist in his aesthetic."[13] On the contrary, it implies that for Hardy, form, like fate, like identity, is as inevitable as it is arbitrary. Though Hardy is entirely arbitrary in his choice of forms, he is incredibly rigorous in his submission to his choice. Form is significant not in itself but only insofar as it battles and gives meaning to freedom; and freedom, in turn, is the means to a saving rediscovery of form. For Hardy, there is no such thing as organic form—there is only an organic *struggle*, and the struggle itself is more important than either of the combatants.

All this is vaguely true for all poets, and it is more of the truth for a poet as exclusively stanzaic as Hardy, but it is pathologically true for one who, like Hardy, both crushes and is crushed by rhythm and shape. It would be ridiculous to suggest that there is a world view common to all stanzaic poets, or even to those few who sound like Hardy, but some striking parallels with George Herbert may clarify the issues at hand.

There is no direct evidence that Hardy knew Herbert's work (and no indirect evidence will be suggested here), though Coleridge, Wordsworth, or Tennyson could easily have led him to one of the fairly numerous nineteenth-century editions and though his love for church music might have acquainted him with the Wesleyan adaptations of Herbert's poems. At any rate, Herbert found his lapidary stanzas a "strict yet welcome size" and conceived of the expansion and constriction of his lines as a kind of tempering process akin to the alternation of wealth and dearth, joy and affliction with which God creates in His people feeling hearts and spiritual resilience. This harmonizes well with Hardy's desire for responsive strength, for emotional reticence—the ability both to feel and to control loss. That Herbert also thinks of the stanza in its Italian sense of room is clear from the tendency of his language to knock up against walls, to be squeezed, to be under great pressure. He too forces accents on whole trains of words:

> How fresh, O Lord, how sweet and clean
> Are thy returns! even as the flowers in spring;
>   To which, besides their own demesne,
> The late-past frosts tributes of pleasure bring.
>     Grief melts away
>     Like snow in May,
>   As if there were no such cold thing.

If Hardy knew this poem, he must certainly have admired the last line of this excerpt with its four consecutive stresses in "no such cold thing." (The weaker fourth line also contains four consecutive stresses.) It is no insult to say that Hardy was rarely capable of such precision, for Herbert's is the most *precise* ear in English poetry, with the possible exceptions of Campion and, in a few of the songs, Shakespeare. Though no one would mistake Herbert for Hardy, their rhythmic assumptions and intentions are nearly identical, and they share a surprising and significant number of other concerns. Both take the dialectic of fate and freedom (Herbert's opposition of divine providence and free will, Hardy's necessity and possibility) as their major theme and follow it closely with an interest in self-deception. Both are deliberately small, homely, and even countrified, and both experiment widely with stanzas. They are fond of church music, architecture, certain recurring words such as "day" and "heart," and the fable (itself a kind of container). Though the analogy is tentative and potentially dangerous, it at least suggests that their particular style may answer to certain emotional and intellectual needs. Coleridge found Herbert to be a great source of comfort, and more than one reader has said the same of Hardy. Herbert's tempering and Hardy's war of necessity and possibility are very close, and their stylistic parallels enforce an interesting comparison.

As much as Hardy is disturbed by the thefts of time, they are his only way of knowing, and as much as he fears what he variously describes as "mechanism," "rote," "form," and so forth, he finds that there is no dancer without the dance. There is considerable ambivalence in his attitude toward poetic shape, and in his preface to the poetry of William Barnes, his clearly self-ignorant detestation of form engenders an interesting half-truth about the function of diction:

> We do not find in the dialect balladists of the seventeenth century, or in Burns (with whom he has sometimes been measured), such careful finish, such verbal dexterities, such searchings for the most cunning syllables, such satisfaction with the best phrase. Had he not begun with dialect, and seen himself recognized as an adept in it before he had quite found himself as a poet, who knows that he might not have brought upon his muse the disaster that has befallen so many earnest versifiers of recent time, have become a slave to the passion for form, and have wasted all his substance in whittling at its shape.
>
> From such, however, he was saved by the conditions of his scene, characters, and vocabulary. It may have been, indeed, that he saw this tendency in himself, and retained the dialect as a corrective to the tendency. Whether or no, by a felicitous instinct he does at times break into sudden irregularities in the midst of his subtle rhythms and measures, as if feeling rebelled against further drill. Then his self-consciousness ends, and his naturalness is saved.[14]

Hardy cared little for criticism, and his own is seldom either very specific or very acute. His indulgence in this elaborate hypothesis on the relationship of diction and individuality is therefore all the more striking, and suggests that he is reading into the lesser poet the dimly perceived lessons of his own experience. The passage is, in fact, less literary criticism than self-analysis, for though Hardy is not a dialect poet, except in the sense that he speaks a dialect of one, what he sees as the function of diction in Barnes applies, at least in part, to his own practice. Hardy's diction is by turns troubling, lively, mechanical, inflated, fresh, wrenching, and perfect, but it is always characteristic in its diversity, and no critic of his poetry, friendly or hostile, can (or does) ignore it. Though Hardy here equates diction with idiosyncrasy, with the escape from necessity and form, it must be said that the line between mechanism and freedom is not easily drawn and that his diction supports his instinct for shaping and mechanizing as often (and usually at the same time) as it furthers his desires for freshness and unpredictability, for it is when we are most personal that we are most habitual.

What critics normally treat, and what we shall consider here, as Hardy's diction is in reality something closer to his undiction, for what we seize upon as typical of Hardy is characterized by its obtrusiveness, its indecorousness, its desire to be atypical. That is, Hardy's words impose upon us most strongly when he is seeking to unsay a context, when, in partial corroboration of his hypothesis, some claustrophobia impels him to reach for what seems the freedom of the unexpected. "The Temporary the All," considered in chapter one, is a good starting point, in that it is an extreme example:

> Change and chancefulness in my flowering youthtime,
> Set me sun by sun near to one unchosen;
> Wrought us fellowlike, and despite divergence,
>     Fused us in friendship.

> [CP5]

There is a strange duplicity in phrases such as "sun by sun" and "wrought us fellowlike" because Hardy is so obviously avoiding the obvious. We read the poem almost as a translation, substituting, though not consciously, "after a time" or "gradually" for "sun by sun," and "made us friends" or "threw us together" for "wrought us fellowlike," and we cannot, in consequence, escape the feeling that the poet is having his own way, is forcing language to disobey itself. The curious paradox of such diction is that it hovers insistently between abbreviation (or terseness) and circumlocution (or inflation) and refuses to be classified as either. In the end the classification is irrelevant, for in either case the effect of the language is to recall what might have been said, what has been replaced, and we are conscious both of a drive for freedom and of the conventional phrasing (even if we do not immediately see what it would have been) which has been avoided.

Terseness and inflation, therefore, function both as reticence and as heightened expression. The abstract solemnity of "despite divergence'' strikes us both as a tactful summary of a long, involved story and as a slightly grandiose way of saying ''though we were different'' or ''though we parted.'' In Hardy's poetry, overstatement and understatement are nearly inseparable and are significant in that they are statements which go over or under an expected statement. ''The Temporary the All'' is abnormal even for Hardy, but it is different in degree, rather than in kind, from his norm. Hardy is constantly struggling to avoid obvious and therefore unfeeling necessities, though the violence of his struggle is not always so apparent. Gentle or violent, his effort is to find ways of responding to the ordinary, to discover the true names of things and actions: ''A very good way of looking at things would be to regard everything as having an actual or false name, and an intrinsic or true name, to ascertain which all endeavour should be made ... The fact is that nearly all things are falsely, or rather inadequately, named.'' (L217)

Hardy is usually at his best when his diction and undiction are virtually indistinguishable, for it seems to be in the nature of language to seem more mechanical the more its inherent mechanisms are resisted, and the wildness of Hardy's freshening possibilities often shades into unfeeling contrivance as he falls back into the hole out of which he is climbing. This is less a denigration of his poetry than a statement of its unalterable condition, for Hardy's sense of diction exhibits the same ambivalences with respect to necessity and possibility as does his concept of form.

Form, as we have seen, is both salvation and death, and when Hardy chides his contemporaries for ''whittling away at its shape,'' we must hear the voice of the master whittler whose obsession with shape is evident even in the oddity and jaggedness of his diction. The very word ''shape'' is sacred to Hardy, and it crops up in unusual and telling contexts:

> On the frigid face of the heath-hemmed pond
>   There shaped the half-grown moon:
> Winged whiffs from the north with a husky croon
>   Blew over and beyond.

[CP676]

Only Hardy could imagine the half moon fingering itself into existence. Here, ''shape'' not only means but functions as shape, for the oddity of its usage calls attention to itself, and the word seems dislocated, like an element in a collage. In Hardy's war with the vague, "shape" is so essential as to be a verb of being or becoming:

> Let thy dreams
> Of me and mine diminish day by day,
> And yield their space to shine of smugger things;
> Till I shape to thee but in fitful gleams,
> And then in far and feeble visitings,
> And then surcease.
>
> [CP58]

> We see by littles now the deft achievement
> Whereby she has escaped the Wrongers all,
> In view of which our momentary breavement
>   Outshapes but small.
>
> [CP254]

> This candle-wax is shaping to a shroud
> To-night. (They call it that, as you may know)—
> By touching it the claimant is avowed,
> And hence I press it with my finger—so . . .
>
> [CP846]

Shape is a claim, the assertion of Hardy's engagement with the vanishing, and his assertion of his control over vaporous language. It is a way of touching for a man who seems to be able to feel the failure to be in the same way that Keats and Browning feel objects. Hardy, for example, seldom uses colors, and when he does we are less conscious of the colors themselves than of the almost tactile strength which has imprisoned them in dullness:

> Its former green is blue and thin,
> And its once firm legs sink in and in;
> Soon it will break down unaware,
> Soon it will break down unaware.

> At night when reddest flowers are black
> Those who once sat thereon came back;
> Quite a row of them sitting there,
> Quite a row of them sitting there.
>
> [CP537]

Colors are not seen, but touched, and when they fade they crumble like rocks:

> I marked her ruined hues,
> Her custom-straitened views,
> And asked, "Can there indwell
>  My Amabel?"
>
> [CP6]

This practice carries over into Hardy's treatment of light. He apprehends and confines it by feeling its rays as prongs and by substituting solidity for brightness, weight for intensity:

> Ancient chalk-pit, milestone, rills in the grass-flat
>  Stroked by the light . . .
>
> [CP285]

> The level flare raked pane and pediment
> And my wrecked face, and shaped my nearing friend . . .
>
> [CP20]

> Never to bid good-bye,
>  Or lip me the softest call,
>  Or utter a wish for a word, while I
> Saw morning harden upon the wall . . .
>
> [CP318]

Perhaps the most pervasive of Hardy's sensual and linguistic solidifications is his employment of nouns, especially nouns representing parts of the body, as verbs:

> So that wherefore should I be here,
>  Watching Adda lip the lea . . .
>
> [CP98]

> Bright yellowhammers
> Made mirthful clamours,
> And billed long straws with a bustling air . . .
>
> [CP311]

> But still she rides gaily
>
> . . . . . . . . . . . . . . . . .
>  And as when first eyed
> Draws rein and sings to the swing of the tide.
>
> [CP333]

> And in the streaming mist
> Fishes might fin a passage if they list.
>
> [CP591]

Again, these usages express shape not only in their fusion of thing and action but through an oddity and dislocation which calls attention to language as a material on which shape is being imposed. Hardy's perception of form is so intense that he can see shaping even in the loss of shape, in the softening of fruit:

> Autumn moulds the hard fruit mellow,
> And forward still we press  . . .
>
> [CP465]

The foregoing examples represent Hardy's desire to replace obvious and therefore unfelt form with the effort of achieved and felt form, and the substitutions he makes in these cases serve as a gloss on many of his oddities of diction. Hardy believes that language must struggle continuously against evaporation, even to the point of becoming ''unpoetic'' in order to assert itself. This is the implication of the conclusion to the elegy for Meredith:

> So that, when now all tongues declare
> His shape unseen by his green hill,
> I scarce believe he sits not there.
>
> No matter. Further and further still
> Through the world's vaporous vitiate air
> His words wing on— as live words will.
>
> [CP280]

The valuation of the poles of vagueness and shape is, however, easily reversed. According to Hardy, the poet is not only the shaper but one who, under the intense pressure of ordinariness, of prefabrication, can call up a saving vagueness, who can ''point out pale phantasmal things, / And talk of vain vague purposings'' (CP355-56). For Hardy, the poet of the rediscovery of patterns, the ugliest threat is the mindless and unquestioned reign of inhuman sameness and repetition in himself and in the universe. He devotes a specialized diction of mechanism to this terrifying prospect:

> Perhaps thy ancient rote-restricted ways
> Thy ripening rule transcends  . . .
>
> [CP172]

> Within the common lamp-lit room
> Prison my eyes and thought;

Let dingy details crudely loom,
  Mechanic speech be wrought . . .
                    [CP201]

    though Time's unflinching rigour,
    In mindless rote, has ruled from sight
  The substance now . . .

                    [CP331]

    to-day is beneaped and stale,
  And its urgent clack
  But a vapid tale.

                    [CP332]

  Where the footstep falls
  With a pit-pat wearisome
  In its cadency
  On the flagstones drearisome . . .
                    [CP535]

  Not a god, but the All
  (As I read); yet a thrall
    To a blind ritual . . .
                    [CP691]

Incomprehensible sameness, numbing repetition, senseless loss, loveless power—these are (like Tennyson's "sad mechanic exercise/ Like dull narcotics, numbing pain") the extremes of necessity and form, and when Hardy veers into their gravitational sphere he is assailed by boredom, horror, and vagueness. Mindless form is as formless as formlessness, and he reacts with shapings which differ from his lippings, wingings, mouthings, and finnings only in their desperation. "Vacant," "dull," "mechanic," "rote," and so forth are words which empty out even as they are shaped. The smallness of this class of words, and the frequency of its occurrence, indicate that it copes with an extreme of repression where the mind can hardly exist. As an attempt to make boredom viable, to make poetic life out of lifelessness, it is the machinery of the most paradoxical of quests.

    This is the point at which necessity ceases to be an impulse, a pole of an opposition, and nearly becomes death, but a less specialized diction of mechanism pervades more manageable and human contexts, as Donald Davie demonstrates in his chapter on Hardy as a "heavy engineer". "The Wind's Prophecy" is a telling example:

I travel on by barren farms,
And gulls glint out like silver flecks
Against a cloud that speaks of wrecks,
And bellies down with black alarms.
I say: "Thus from my lady's arms
I go; those arms I love the best!"
The wind replies from dip and rise,
"Nay; toward her arms thou journeyest."

A distant verge morosely gray
Appears, while clots of flying foam
Break from its muddy monochrome,
And a light blinks up far away.
I sigh: "My eyes now as all day
Behold her ebon loops of hair!"
Like bursting bonds the wind responds,
"Nay, wait for tresses flashing fair!"

From tides the lofty coastlands screen
Come smitings like the slam of doors,
Or hammerings on hollow floors,
As the swell cleaves through caves unseen.
Say I: "Though broad this wild terrene
Her city home is matched of none!"
From the hoarse skies the wind replies:
"Thou shouldst have said her sea-bord one."

The all-prevailing clouds exclude
The one quick timorous transient star;
The waves outside where breakers are
Huzza like a mad multitude.
"Where the sun ups it, mist-imbued,"
I cry, "there reigns the star for me!"
The wind outshrieks from points and peaks:
"Here, westward, where it downs, mean ye!"

Yonder the headland, vulturine,
Snores like old Skrymer in his sleep,
And every chasm and every steep
Blackens as wakes each pharos-shine
"I roam, but one is safely mine,"
I say. "God grant she stay my own!"
Low laughs the wind as if it grinned:

"Thy Love is one thou'st not yet known."

[CP464]

Davie's exposition of the potential for mechanism in this apparently innocent poem is perceptive:

> What is uncanny is the way the elements are made to menace the traveler, and through associations with technology—the gulls "glint" with a metallic glitter; when the sea comes into sight, its "muddy monochrome" has a hint of the daguerrotype; and when the sea passes out of sight, the sound it makes is a slamming and a hammering. These industrial associations gather until we wonder whether the huzza-ing multitude of the penultimate stanza is not a dangerously mercurial proletariat.

This is excellent, but in order to account for what he calls "the inexplicable urgency and ominousness of the poem," Davie (tentatively, it is true) hypothesizes that Hardy is guilty about his exchange of lovers and feels that he is a "class traitor." The analysis concludes with "it is as if what separated Hardy from Tryphena was the Industrial Revolution itself, or at least as if the nature which divided them . . . were itself a massive machine."[15] It is perhaps possible to develop Davie's observations using the categories established in this and the preceding chapters.

"The Wind's Prophecy" is a collocation of five typical Hardy poems, and there is some doubt, as Davie notes, that it works as a whole. At any rate, the poem deals with possibilities in the process of being lost, and it is characterized by the division of awareness which is so fundamentally Hardy's. Each stanza proceeds from natural description to past ignorance (the present tense of the poem) to present knowledge (the prophecy of the wind) that Hardy has temporarily unknown. The pattern is familiar, and we can take the initial stanza as a paradigm. As is usual in Hardy, the accumulation of natural detail creates a sense of incompleteness, a sense of the exclusion or repression of the human. The landscape is, in fact, repressed—the farms are barren, the glinting gulls are dwindling into winged machines—and, as usual, this repression or delay shades into omen: "a cloud that speaks of wrecks." With the introduction of "wrecks," the return of the human is triggered, and a self emerges, defining itself, as in the poems considered in the previous

chapter, in terms of its limits, its ignorance. The unknowing speaker
sees the ominousness of the landscape as appropriate to his departure
from his lover, but the poem divides, moving from involvement to
ironic knowledge, and the wind repeatedly asserts the irrelevance of
the omen—the speaker is actually *approaching* his true love. Each of
the five stanzas follows the same pattern. A reduced, narrowed, and
manipulated landscape, described with the diction of mechanism,
wells up into omen—a light or the absence of a light. The speaker
misinterprets and the wind reinterprets. The wind becomes a symbol
for the shift in awareness, and it would be easy to see it as the
equivalent of time. The poem is one of Hardy's most windblown
productions, and we may partially explain this in terms of the energy
released by the exclusions and explosions of each of the five stanzas.

All the omens turn out to be false except insofar as they predict a
new perspective, and the poem becomes an assertion of the relevance
of irrelevance. In the end, it will not do to attach its ''ominousness''
to anything so specific as Hardy's social misgivings upon the
abandonment of a lover, for omen is so ubiquitous a phenomenon in
Hardy's poetry that it clings more generally to any division of
awareness. It is one of fate's, and Hardy's, favorite tricks to present us
with unmistakeable omens which are mistakes, which are significant
not for what they seem to tell but rather for their own ominousness.
They signal a delay, a pending completion or change of awareness,
an onrushing necessity.

''Overlooking the River Stour'' is top-heavy, and therefore less
typical in movement, but it, too, is cited by Davie as an example of
Hardy's heavy engineering, and it will further this argument:

> The swallows flew in the curves of an eight
>   Above the river-gleam
>   In the wet June's last beam:
> Like little crossbows animate
> The swallows flew in the curves of an eight
>   Above the river-gleam.
>
> Planing up shavings of crystal spray
>   A moor-hen darted out
>   From the bank thereabout,
> And through the stream-shine ripped his way;
> Planing up shavings of crystal spray
>   A moor-hen darted out.

Closed were the kingcups; and the mead
 Dripped in monotonous green
 Though the day's morning sheen
Had shown it golden and honeybee'd;
Closed were the kingcups; and the mead
 Dripped in monotonous green.

And never I turned my head, alack,
 While these things met my gaze
 Through the pane's drop-drenched glaze,
To see the more behind my back....
O never I turned, but let, alack,
 These less things hold my gaze!

[CP452–53]

Davie, again, has perceptive comments:

> For whereas the poem presents itself as three stanzas
> running in parallel, with a last stanza that turns back upon
> them all, in fact we experience a notable shift between the
> second stanza and the third. In the first two stanzas live
> creatures, the birds, are transformed into machines: the
> swallows into crossbows, and the moor-hen into some sort
> of lathe. (For the double sense of "planing" is decisively
> tipped toward its mechanic sense by "ripped" and "shav-
> ings.") In the third stanza, however, the kingcups are
> presented in normal organic terms. The shift is notable.
> And yet the poet gives no indication that he has noticed it.[16]

In this poem, Hardy must sustain his useful boredom, his
mechanistic repression, through nearly four stanzas (as opposed to
four *lines* in each of the stanzas of "The Wind's Prophecy"), and
characteristically, the means he chooses is the monotony of repetition. If in the third stanza he ceases to describe nature as a machine,
it is probably because the threatening diction of mechanism is beginning to fall of its own weight by the time of the repeated line
"Dripped in monotonous green." It begins to recall, through its
own persistence, another perspective and another time: "Though
the day's morning sheen/Had shown it golden ..." Even the
closed kingcups hint at a disclosure. Soon the elaborate concentration on the scene is blown apart by its own irrelevance. The self pre-
cipitates in the final stanza, and the nature and consequences of the

exclusion of the human become so painfully clear that we need no wind to prophesy.

Davie is absolutely correct in asserting that Hardy has in him the makings of a Victorian technician, and we need only add that Hardy has assimilated these apparently unpromising elements not for themselves but rather because they correspond to one pole or impulse of the poetic process. They occur in association with the dominance of form and necessity, with the creative repression or unknowing of the self and of the human.

These unceasing transitions between states of awareness account for the final noticeable element of Hardy's style that we shall consider, an element which he seems to share with Shelley—that is, a fondness for negative constructions:

> Some one charm the world unknows . . .
> > [CP132]

> One who, past doubtings all,
> > Waits in unhope . . .
> > > [CP153]

> I cannot bear my fate as writ,
> > I'd have my life unbe . . .
> > > [CP162]

> 'Tis not that we have unforetold
> > The drop behind . . .
> > > [CP133]

> Had the house-front been glass,
> > My vision unobscuring . . .
> > > [CP422]

> My head unturned lest my dream should fade.
> > [CP498]

> > This whole day long I unfulfil.
> > > [CP548]

> > Taking his life's stern stewardship
> > With blithe uncare . . .
> > > [CP678]

> > That shepherd still stands in that white smock-frock,
> > Unnoting all things save the counting his flock.
> > > [CP803]

Of such usages C. H. Salter says, "The general explanation of the frequency of negatives in Hardy is his negative attitude toward life,"[17] but this is surely an oversimplification. Shelley's negatives tend to be adjectives, and they describe what is not, or what cannot be described. Most of Hardy's are verbs, or verbals, and they generally refer to states of mind or being—unbe, unknow, unhope, unvision, unsight, unconscious, uncare. They constitute the boundary between two states of awareness, two perspectives. "Unknows," for example, is a more powerful and dynamic way of saying "forgets" or "does not notice," and the significance of the coinage is surely that it expresses Hardy's sense of the dialectical or antinomian relationship between awareness and ignorance, involvement and distance, that is, between two possible selves. Forgetting is not merely the absence of memory but rather its denial or repression. It is a process, a deliberate exclusion, a negative vector rather than zero.

Hardy's negative verbals are another result of his minute and insistent changes of perspective and awareness. His poetry seldom achieves a Romantic intensity because his intensity consistently short-circuits itself. It becomes self-conscious, and this self-consciousness soon burgeons into another self, an ironic or qualifying awareness which completes or complements what has gone before. Hardy seeks to believe only in his own division, but division is de-vision, and it is by nature an untenable repression. Vision returns, as it must, through the back door, and though Hardy does not believe in it, it believes in him. He is haunted by himself.

# 4
## OLD FURNITURE:
## HARDY'S WORLD

I see the hands of the generations
  That owned each shiny familiar thing
In play on its knobs and indentations,
  And with its ancient fashioning
  Still dallying:

Hands behind hands, growing paler and paler,
  As in a mirror a candle flame
Shows images of itself, each frailer
  As it recedes . . .

"Old Furniture" CP456

"The world does not despise us; it only neglects us" (L48)—so Hardy wrote in his twenty-fifth year, and so he labored to believe for the rest of his life, but it was an impossible faith. The man who could not himself be indifferent could neither accept nor fathom indifference in any quarter, and the stony neutrality of the universe kept dressing itself up as mindless malignity, helpless love, and tragic indecision. Part of Hardy tried desperately to take only what the cosmos unequivocally gave, but he heard voices he could not be sure were his own. Beset by omens and ghosts, haunted by the past and by his own divisions, he could not escape the feeling that the universe was on the verge of uttering itself, and he sought to help it along. The words never came, but Hardy never stopped listening.

Hardy saw himself as the heroic unbeliever, and he was true to himself in that he could not even believe in unbelief. Though he was fascinated by his own explanations, they were not, and could not be, enough, and his life work was the praise of the inexplicable. When in 1920 he was queried for information for a projected *Biographical Dictionary of Modern Rationalists,* he replied, with a characteristic mixture of condescension and envy, that he was forced to exclude himself, along with the rest of the human race, from that hopeful and hopeless company:

> As Mr. Hardy has a cold which makes writing trying to his eyes, I answer your letter for him. He says he thinks he is rather an irrationalist than a rationalist, on account of his inconsistencies. He has, in fact, declared as much in the prefaces to some of his poems, where he explains his views as being mere impressions that frequently change. Moreover, he thinks he could show that no man is a rationalist, and that human actions are not ruled by reason at all in the last resort. But this, of course, is outside the question. So that he cannot honestly claim to belong to the honorable body you are including in your dictionary, whom he admires for their straightforward sincerity and permanent convictions, though he does not quite think they can claim their title. (L403)

What we sometimes perceive as Hardy's rationalism is in reality a species of functional rationalization. It is deep and serious parody. For all his meticulous concern with the sequence of events, he begins where the trail of causality vanishes into the underlife, where a man, in a fatal moment of vast and magical self-detachment, sells his wife or falls in love, commits "a deed of hell"—

> And lo, there in my view
> Pressed against an upper lattice
> Was a white face gazing at us
> As we withdrew.
>
> And well did I divine
> It to be the man's there dying,
> Who but lately had been sighing
> For her pledged mine.
>
> Then I deigned a deed of hell;
> It was done before I knew it;
> What devil made me do it
> I cannot tell!
>
> Yes, while he gazed above,
> I put my arm around her
> That he might see, nor doubt her
> My plighted Love.
>
> [CP298]

—or, as in "The Thing Unplanned," a superhuman, if not a divine, act:

> The white winter sun struck its note on the bridge,
>   The meadow-rills rippled and gleamed
> As I left the thatched post-office, just by the ridge,
> And dropped in my pocket her long tender letter,
> With: "This must be snapped! it is more than it seemed;
>   And now is the opportune time!"
>
> But against what I willed worked the surging sublime
>   Of the thing that I did—the thing better!
>
> [CP750]

Faced with the paradoxes of human motivation, the rationalist must confess himself as helpless as the poet, but Hardy's powerlessness is willful and cultivated, for there are many things he desires to unknow. In the end, he wishes not to explain or judge but to sympathize with those manhandled by the inexplicable or by their own tragic ignorance, and he will not allow anyone or anything to be set up for any but the most ghastly laughter. His view of his "humor" is almost as revealing as it is strange:

> Lastly, Hardy had a born sense of humour, even a too keen sense occasionally: but his poetry was sometimes placed by editors in the hands of reviewers deficient in that quality. Even if they were accustomed to Dickensian humour they were not to Swiftian. Hence it unfortunately happened that verses of a satirical, dry, caustic, or farcical cast were regarded by them with deepest seriousness. In one case the tragic nature of his verse was instanced by the ballad called 'The Bride-night Fire,' or 'The Fire at Tranter Sweatley's,' the criticism being by an accomplished old friend of his own, Frederic Harrison, who deplored the painful nature of the bridegroom's end in leaving only a bone behind him. This piece of work Hardy had written and published when quite a young man, and had hesitated to reprint because of its too pronounced obviousness as a jest. (L302)

The poem in question is not good enough to be tragic, but neither is it, despite its jog-trot, thick dialect, and wild plot, funny, though an attempt at humor would perhaps account for some of the confusion of its aims. This misjudgment on Hardy's part is by no means isolated. After finishing *Human Shows*, many a reader must page backwards in astonishment upon learning in the preface to the next volume that Hardy felt he had been "too liberal in admitting flippant, not to say farcical, pieces" (CP793) into the earlier collection. Hardy's invocation of Swift is, of course, purely fantastic. If, like Swift, he can magnify or minimize his subjects, what he discovers in doing so is not grotesque self-importance but incongruity and poignance. Hardy can easily see how things *could* have been, but he does not blame men for the way they are, and the phrase "should have been" has practically no meaning for him. For all his feeling for the disparities of the cosmos, Hardy has little sense of the absurdity of men. He writes *Satires of Circumstance*, but circumstances make not for satire but for an invocation of frustration, futility, and incongruity which is seldom amenable to humor: " 'All is vanity,' saith the Preacher. But if all were only vanity, who would mind? Alas, it is too often worse than vanity; agony, darkness, death also" (L112). When he wields his version of the poison pen, Hardy is a weak writer. The necessity of unremitting distance confuses him, and consequently he is neither humorous nor tragic. His jokes belong to the cosmos, and their punch lines are blows that strike without regard to desert. All in all, the rationalism inherent in Hardy's plotting and character motivation is a kind of pseudo-explanation whose function is to grow more and more inadequate to our responses as it works itself out. It is one of those imposed forms that he needs, and must battle, in order to feel.

In most areas, however, Hardy is not even apparently rationalistic, and he is repeatedly, and with some justice, cited as an example of a religious man without a religion. The *Life*, which despite its colorless pronouncements, its parade of the great, and its endless guest lists, has some claim to be considered as a work of the imagination (or at least as an essay in one of Hardy's favorite art forms—the headstone), reveals a predisposition to superstition, which though certainly not abnormal, is significant. As a boy, Hardy was fond of chanting the hymn "And now another day is gone" when the sunset fired the Venetian red walls of the staircase at Bockhampton (L15), and he professed not to "think much of *Hamlet* because the ghost did not play his part up to the end as he ought to have done" (L24). An intention to enter the clergy persisted well into his young manhood. All this is important only insofar as it predicts what Samuel Hynes calls "the superstitious sense of terrible knowledge"[1] which permeates the poetry of the older Hardy, despite the godlessness of his universe. Hardy is "A Sign-Seeker":

> —There are who, rapt to heights of trancelike trust,
>   These tokens claim to feel and see,
>   Read radiant hints of times to be—
> Of heart to heart returning after dust to dust.
>
> Such scope is granted not to lives like mine...
>   I have lain in dead men's beds, have walked
>   The tombs of those with whom I had talked,
> Called many a gone and goodly one to shape a sign...
>
> [CP 44]

Echoing the second paragraph of *Alastor*, Hardy laments never having been visited, but his desire rather than his failure defines him. One is tempted, for example, to see the story of Hardy's maternal grandmother and her father as a kind of paradigm for the conflicting claims of saving imagination and tyrannical reason:

> Her bright intelligence in a literary direction did not serve her in domestic life. After her mother's death she clandestinely married a young man of whom her father strongly disapproved. The sturdy yeoman, apparently a severe and unyielding parent, never forgave her, and never would see her again. His unbending temper is illustrated by the only anecdote known of him. A fortune-telling gypsy had encamped on the edge of one of his fields, and on a Sunday morning he went to order her away. Finding her obdurate he said: 'If you don't take yourself off I'll have you burnt as a witch!' She pulled his handkerchief from his pocket, and threw it into her fire, saying, 'If that burn I burn.' The flames curled up round the handkerchief, which was his best, of India silk, but it did not burn, and she handed it back to him intact. The tale goes that he was so impressed by her magic that he left her alone. (L7)

Hardy does not "believe" this story, any more than he believes the legend of "The Oxen":

> Christmas Eve, and twelve of the clock.
> "Now they are all on their knees,"
> An elder said as we sat in a flock
> By the embers in hearthside ease.

We pictured the meek mild creatures where
   They dwelt in their strawy pen,
Nor did it occur to one of us there
   To doubt they were kneeling then.

So fair a fancy few would weave
   In these years! Yet, I feel
If someone said on Christmas Eve,
   "Come; see the oxen kneel

"In the lonely barton by yonder coomb
   Our childhood used to know,"
I should go with him in the gloom,
   Hoping it might be so.

                            [CP439]

As Delmore Schwartz notes, however, the subtraction of either the possibility for belief or the necessity of disbelief from the poem would unbalance its crucial division of awareness and destroy its poignance.[2] Hardy holds knowing and unknowing, disbelief and belief, in colloidal suspension, though this is decreasingly true as the faith in question approaches the forms of orthodox Christianity, which normally polarize him into polemic.

Hardy creates a religion of nostalgia, a communal rite of memory. He is haunted by the ghost of his own division, and when he listens for signs he hears the echoes of his own listening and calls them the universe's belief in him. Life becomes a phantasmal ceremony, and he is unable to dismiss its intuitions and coincidences, unable to be sure the voices which come to him are indeed his own:

> In the train on the way to London. Wrote the first four or six lines of "Not a line of her writing have I." It was a curious instance of sympathetic telepathy. The woman whom I was thinking of—a cousin—was dying at the time, and I quite in ignorance of it. She died six days later. The remainder of the piece was not written till after her death. (L224)

Hardy has traded the life of "faith diversified by doubt" for that of "doubt diversified by faith," and though his self-division makes single-minded credulity embarrassing and impossible, it also

110

undermines all but the easiest of skepticisms:

> Half my time—particularly when writing verse—I "believe" (in the modern sense of the word) not only in the things Bergson believes in, but in spectres, mysterious voices, intuitions, omens, dreams, haunted places, etc., etc. But I do not believe in them in the old sense of the word any more for that. (L370)

The "old sense of the word," if indeed there ever was one, glimmers feebly on the far side of the chasm which is Hardy's diminution, his division. The simple verb becomes a dialectic of believing and unbelieving, of tentative approach and tentative withdrawal, of attempted rationalization and heroic unknowing.

Hardy's specters, intuitions, voices, and omens are the complaints of the forgotten. They warn of the passing of the present and strive against the pastness of the past. The dead must return, for the disappearance of their possibilities imprisons us in the overpowering necessity of the moment. For Hardy, the fading of the past is therefore a far more pressing emergency than the disappearance of God—except insofar as it is the *same* emergency. The postulate "I remember, therefore I am," which James Kissane sees as underlying Tennyson's "passion of the past" is fundamental to Hardy as well.[3] The past, not the supreme being, gives us meaning and identity, and its persistence is our persistence, our immortality: "Today has length, breadth, thickness, colour, smell, voice. As soon as it becomes *yesterday* it is a thin layer among many layers, without substance, colour, or articulate sound" (L285). It is curious that Hardy felt it necessary to qualify "without sound" with "articulate." This apparition of yesterday is all we have, and it is trying to speak, but it must be caressed into significance. The present belongs to itself, but memory is ours and we are memory. When "The Absolute Explains," it explains that being, presence, is eternal, and that the past is another place to live:

> I
> "O no," said It: her lifedoings
>   Time's touch hath not destroyed:
> They lie their length, with the throbbing things
>   Akin them, down the Void,
>   Live, unalloyed.

II
"Know, Time is toothless, seen all through;
　The Present, that men but see,
Is phasmal: since in a sane purview
　All things are shaped to be
　　Eternally.

. . . . . . . . . . . . . . . . . . . . . . . . . . . . . . . . . .

XV
"And hence, of her you asked about
　At your first speaking: she
Hath, I assure you, not passed out
　Of continuity,
　　But is in me.

XVI
"So thus doth Being's length transcend
　Time's ancient regal claim
To see all lengths begin and end.
　'The Fourth Dimension' fame
　　Bruits as its name."

[CP716-19]

If Hardy believes anything, he believes this, or rather, he thinks,
feels, and acts as if it might and must be true. He even seeks a
rational basis for his faith, poignantly enlisting Einstein as an
unanswerable ally: "Relativity. That things and events always were,
are, and will be (e.g. Emma, Mother and Father are living still in
the past)" (L 419).

The Present dies despite us, but when, as Swinburne says,
"death lies dead," the past calls out to be saved. Hardy's
powerlessness is in the present, which somehow must be what it is,
not in the past, which somehow could have been otherwise. He
only knows and possesses what is gone. Tennyson's "to have loved
and lost" becomes nearly tautological, for love *is* loss, and the
attempt to love everything is the attempt to *be* no one. All this
accounts for what is surely the most striking passage in the *Life*:

> For my part, if there is any way of getting a melancholy satis-
> faction out of life it lies in dying, so to speak, before one is
> out of the flesh; by which I mean putting on the manners
> of ghosts, wandering in their haunts, and taking their

views of surrounding things. To think of life as passing away is a sadness; to think of it as past is at least tolerable. Hence even when I enter into a room to pay a simple morning call I have unconsciously the habit of regarding the scene as if I were a spectre not solid enough to influence my environment; only fit to behold and say, as another spectre said: "Peace be unto you!" (L209-10)

The desire to be a ghostly and powerless observer of the fleeting moment finds a curious parallel in Ruskin's *Praeterita* (vol. 1, chap. 9):

My entire delight was in observing without being myself noticed,—if I could have been invisible, all the better. I was absolutely interested in men and their ways, as I was interested in marmots and chamois, in tomtits and trout. If only they would stay still and let me look at them, and not get into their holes and up their heights! The living inhabitation of the world—the grazing and nesting in it,—the spiritual power of the air, the rocks, the waters, to be in the midst of it, and rejoice and wonder at it, and help it if I could,—happier if it needed no help of mine.

Here Ruskin, like Hardy, reacts to the speed and demands of the present by imagining himself as a spectral voyeur, knowing and loving, but preferably powerless to "help." He does not explicitly make the Hardyan connection between this detachment and his own pastness, but it is only a short step from Ruskin's desire for a slower and more independent present to Hardy's home in the past. Both are symptoms of self-division, but Hardy's, as in the portrait of his paternal grandmother (according to J. O. Bailey) in "One We Knew," is expressed in temporal terms:[4]

> She seemed one left behind of a band gone distant
>   So far that no tongue could hail:
> Past things retold were to her as things existent,
>   Things present but as a tale.
>
> [CP258]

The presence of the past is inextricably intertwined with the pastness of the present. To the extent that Hardy's ghosts are his other selves, they signal the preservation of possibility, the return of the past. To the extent that he himself is a ghost, he is defending against the garish and chaotic possibilities of the present through his own abdication, becoming powerful through the surrender of power, possessing again by losing.

The wildness of the present is closely related to Hardy's intense homeliness. As we found the examination of some of the "Poems of Pilgrimage," Hardy makes himself comfortable in a place by finding the part of it which belongs to him, the point at which its memories touch his, and he is unable to face the United States, a land of the vivid present, a land lacking "that long drip of human tears" (CP99). Hardy's homeliness, his accommodation of past and present, is perfectly illustrated by "the earliest discoverable of the young Hardy's attempts at verse," printed in the *Life*, dated there "between 1857 and 1860," and entitled, conveniently enough for this argument, "Domicilium":

> It faces west, and round the back and sides
> High beeches, bending, hang a veil of boughs,
> And sweep against the roof. Wild honeysucks
> Climb on the walls, and seem to sprout a wish
> (If we may fancy wish of trees and plants)
> To overtop the apple-trees hard by.
>
> Red roses, lilacs, variegated box
> Are there in plenty, and such hardy flowers
> As flourish best untrained. Adjoining these
> Are herbs and esculents; and farther still
> A field; then cottages with trees, and last
> The distant hills and sky.
>
> Behind, the scene is wilder. Heath and furze
> Are everything that seems to grow and thrive
> Upon the uneven ground. A stunted thorn
> Stands here and there, indeed; and from a pit
> An oak uprises, springing from a seed
> Dropped by some bird a hundred years ago.
>
> In days bygone—
> Long gone—my father's mother, who is now
> Blest with the blest, would take me out to walk.
> At such a time I once inquired of her
> How looked the spot when first she settled here.

The answer I remember. 'Fifty years
Have passed since then, my child, and change has marked
The face of all things. Yonder garden-plots
And orchards were uncultivated slopes
O'ergrown with bramble bushes, furze and thorn:
That road a narrow path shut in by ferns,
Which, almost trees, obscured the passer-by.

'Our house stood quite alone, and those tall firs
And beeches were not planted. Snakes and efts
Swarmed in the summer days, and nightly bats
Would fly about our bedrooms. Heathcroppers
Lived on the hills, and were our only friends;
So wild it was when first we settled here.'

[L4]

The controlling opposition of this Wordsworthian piece (which sounds so much older and more formal than the mature Hardy—only the young are older than the old) is that between domesticity and wildness, human presence or memory and natural chaos. What is near the house is given shape—the beeches "veil" the scene, the honeysuckle clings to the wall, and even the untamed, "hardy" flowers ("hardy" is a word which describes both the poet and his poems, but which he seldom uses) suggest the presence of the Hardys—but we move quickly to the distance and the vastness of the hills and sky. Behind the house, hidden from the glow of its countenance, are wilder scenes, which Hardy, in obedience to Wordsworth though with some distress, inventories, until he rests in the discovery of the past of an oak—the seed "dropped by some bird a hundred years ago." This seems to trigger the second half of the poem, which is doubly distanced and doubly possessed in that it is a reminiscence of a reminiscence. It qualifies the threatening wildness of the first half by reminding Hardy that what he sees is in fact the product of a long domestication of an even greater wildness. There is perhaps no true ghost in this poem, but its invocation of the past characteristically both deepens and denies the present.

In his unremitting search for home and comfort in the universe, Hardy finds the handholds of human memory, and it is both remarkable and inevitable that a man who is practically bodiless in the present should have such a vivid sense of touch in the past:

That floor, of every colour and rich device, is worn into undulations by the infinite multitudes of feet that have trodden it, and *what* feet there have been among the rest! (L193)

The keenness was gone from the mouldings of the doorways, but whether worn out by the rubbing past of innumerable people's shoulders, and the moving of their heavy furniture, or by Time in a grander and more abstract form, did not appear.[5]

Hardy needs a world where all time persists, and the sight of human wear and tear is his door out of a present which is simultaneously void and suffocating. He possesses presence, but is burdened by the present. For him, memory is the source of all character, as is evident when an old dwelling speaks to a new one in "The Two Houses":

> "You have not known
> Men's lives, deaths, toils, and teens;
> You are but a heap of stick and stone:
> A new house has no sense of the have-beens.
>
> "Void as a drum
> You stand: I am packed with these,
> Though, strangely, living dwellers who come
> See not the phantoms all my substance sees!
>
> "Visible in the morning
> Stand they, when dawn drags in;
> Visible at night; yet hint or warning
> Of these thin elbowers few of the inmates win.
>
> . . . . . . . . . . . . . . . . . . . . . . . . . . . . . . . . .
>
> "Where such inbe,
> A dwelling's character
> Takes theirs, and a vague semblancy
> To them in all its limbs, and light, and atmosphere.
>
> [CP564]

What is new, what is irredeemably present, is merely a heap, but what is ancient shapes itself into "elbowers," into characters and lives.

Because the past is always present, Hardy is intensely, even superstitiously, excited by coincidences in space. He is drawn to the graves of poets and other ancestors; he speculates that he and his mother have stayed in a room once occupied by Shelley; he writes a poem about Keats's brief sojourn in Dorset on the way to Rome and then finds himself on a committee whose purpose is to acquire one of Keats's homes. Space, too, can be collapsed, and when it is, he is concerned with coincidence in time: "It bridges over the years a little to think that Gray might have seen Wordsworth in his cradle, and Wordsworth might have seen me in mine." (L386).

All memory is sacred, and Hardy cares for it as for a nearly extinct species. Though he appears to have been especially close to no one in his life, he finds staunch friends in the dead, even in dead enemies:

> "... On the Pacific coast
> I have vowed for long that relics of my forbears
>   I'd trace ere lost,
>
> "And hitherward I come,
> Before this same old Time shall strike me numb,
> To carry it out."—"Strange, this is!" said the other
>   "What mind shall plumb
>
> "Coincident design!
> Though these my father's enemies were and mine,
> I nourished a like purpose—to restore them
>   Each letter and line."
>
> [CP362–63]

This describes the action of a fictional character, but Hardy himself appears to have gone to great lengths to accommodate the memory of the dead, and he even designed a tool to assist him in his efforts:

> The many pilgrimages Hardy made with his wife to Stinsford Church took place usually in the evening during the summer, and in the afternoon during the winter. On October 9, however, contrary to his usual custom, he walked to Stinsford in the morning. The bright sunlight shone across the face of a worn tomb whose lettering Hardy had often endeavoured to decipher, so that he might recarve the letters with his penknife. (L428)

> We drove in the afternoon to Stinsford, to put flowers on the family graves. The tombs were very green, being

covered with moss because they are under a yew-tree. T. H. scraped off most of the moss with a little wooden implement like a toy spade, six inches in length, which he made with his own hands and which he carries in his pocket when he goes to Stinsford. He remarked that Walter de la Mare had told him that he preferred to see the gravestones green. (L442)

Though Hardy is intellectually convinced of the neutrality of the universe, that neutrality, in the end, becomes ominous and speaks of hidden or inarticulate human meaning. Indeed, he links the faculty which sees "enemies, etc., in inanimate objects" to his sense of omen by calling it "apprehension," and fixes it with respect to his self-division by defining it as a "semi-madness" (L204). Under the intense domesticating stare of the poet, nothing can remain indifferent, and reality either flees or approaches, rejects or embraces us—usually simultaneously. It both admits to being our home and refuses to live with anyone. Each perception, therefore, divides us into recognition and alienation, desire and reluctance, present and absent selves, or as Hardy once, quite penetratingly, defined the division, into pleasure and pain: "In time one might get to regard every object, and every action, as composed, not of this or that material, this or that movement, but of the qualities of pleasure and pain in varying proportions" (L217).

This, it may be, is Hardy's home-grown version of utilitarianism, but it is certainly his statement of the inescapable condition of consciousness. In his use of this opposition to characterize his division, his sense of friendliness and otherness, Hardy hints at his relationship to minds as apparently alien to him as Swinburne and D. G. Rossetti. Though he denies the humanity of nature, he cannot "help noting countenances in objects of scenery" (L285). All matter becomes sentient, though the faces he sees and the voices he hears are his own, leaping from behind the arras of the forgotten or unknown:

> That mirror
> Whose magic penetrates like a dart
> Who lifts that mirror

> And throws our mind back on us, and our heart,
> > Until we start?

[CP401]

This is the jest of self-division. Listening in, listening *at*, the void, Hardy hears the footfalls of his own return and is, like Sludge, assailed by omens:

> Then, sir, suppose I can, and will, and do
> Look microscopically as is right,
> Into each hour with its infinitude
> Of influences at work to profit Sludge?
> For that's the case: I've sharpened up my sight
> To spy a providence in the fire's going out,
> The kettle's boiling, the dime's sticking fast
> Despite the hole i' the pocket. Call such facts
> Fancies, too petty a work for Providence.
> . . . . . . . . . . . . . . . . . . . . . . . . . . . . . . . . . . . .
> I'm eyes, ears, mouth of me, one gaze and gape,
> Nothing eludes me, everything's a hint,
> Handle and help. It's all absurd, and yet
> There's something in it all, I know: how much?

[B407]

The "microscopic" nature of this vision is important, for it seems that the self is divided when it tries, ultimately unsuccessfully, to submit to the particular, to concentrate its entirety on an unwilling detail or quality of its surroundings. A kind of leakage occurs, and the momentary concentration is overturned by the buffeting of larger possibilities of sentience, by the sense of absent presence, which somehow attaches itself to the detail in question. The self is comforted by itself, and finds an elusive friend in its own division: "I sit under a tree, and feel alone: I think of certain insects around me as magnified by the microscope: creatures like elephants, flying dragons, etc. And I feel I am by no means alone" (L107). This is the working of the underlife, the water table of consciousness which is always welling up and streaming out into the light, where its far gleams become the gestures of an inarticulate world. When Hardy is most alone, he forges a community of presence, of touch, and he attributes the solidity of matter to a joining of hands. The forgotten

119

wander from oblivion and the dead "creep underground" (CP322). Frequently, Hardy's vision is not merely microscopic but molecular, and the infinitesimal fragments of the dead retain their presence, their sense of touch, even their identity. This is the case in "Voices from Things Growing in a Churchyard" (CP590) and in "Transformations," one of his very greatest poems:

> Portion of this yew
> Is a man my grandsire knew,
> Bosomed here at its foot:
> This branch may be his wife,
> A ruddy human life
> Now turned to a green shoot.
>
> These grasses must be made
> Of her who often prayed,
> Last century, for repose;
> And the fair girl long ago
> Whom I often tried to know
> May be entering this rose.
>
> So, they are not underground,
> But as nerves and veins abound
> In the growths of upper air,
> And they feel the sun and the rain,
> And the energy again
> That made them what they were!
>
> [CP443]

It is true, as Hynes remarks, that Hardy attempted to cleave to "monistic materialism"[6]—but see what magnificent spiritualism he has made of it! The past fights its way to its own energy, struggles back into human awareness, back into its immortality. That this idea, or rather feeling, was especially close to Hardy is implied by the fact that it inspires one of the few interesting poems in the generally bland, posthumous *Winter Words* (1928). Though we cannot be sure of the date of "Proud Songsters," its publication in the *Daily Telegraph* of April 9, 1928[7] suggests that it is late, as does its looseness relative to the masterful "Transformations":

> The thrushes sing as the sun is going,
> And the finches whistle in ones and pairs,

And as it gets dark loud nightingales
   In bushes
Pipe, as they can when April wears,
   As if all time were theirs.

These are brand-new birds of twelve-months' growing,
Which a year ago, or less than twain,
No finches were, nor nightingales,
   Nor thrushes,
But only particles of grain,
   And earth, and air, and rain.

[CP797–98]

Matter summons itself into life, and the mere repetition of elements—"earth, and air, and rain"—shakes with light.

For Hardy, as for Browning's Caliban, the supreme entity of the cosmos is the Quiet, Jehovah being only one of the many anthropomorphic mistranslations of silence. The Quiet, however, is ominous, and what Hardy repeatedly attempts to see as its growing self-awareness is a reflection of his own struggle to become aware of it. The speaker creates the listener, and the listener, in turn, creates the speaker. When Hardy reaches into the mirror, the mirror, though reluctantly, reaches back. For him, the Quiet is the past (the dead, the forgotten, the unknown), and its translations (or mistranslations) are the ghosts and voices of his poetry. Accordingly, Hardy's attitudes toward the dead are a crucial gloss on his sense of the universe and of himself. "Friends Beyond," from *Wessex Poems*, provides an early and illuminating example:

William Dewy, Tranter Reuben, Farmer Ledlow late at plough,
  Robert's kin, and John's, and Ned's,
And the Squire, and Lady Susan, lie in Mellstock churchyard now!
"Gone," I call them, gone for good, that group of local
                    hearts and heads;
  Yet at mothy curfew-tide,
And at midnight when the noon-heat breathes it back
               from walls and leads,
They've a way of whispering to me—fellow-wight who yet abide—
  In the muted, measured note
Of a ripple under archways, or a lone cave's stillicide . . .

[CP52–53]

The poet is the listener; what he strives to hear is the message that "gone" does not mean "gone for good." It is significant that the image preceding the voices of the dead is of a cold present ("midnight") redeemed and brought into focus by the warmth of what is past ("noon-heat breathes it back from walls"), and that the noiseless breathing shades imperceptibly into whispering. The ghostly warmth suggests the approach of a body, and the voices are torn from a suspenseful silence made maddening by "muted, measured" interruptions like the barely audible dripping faucets (here, a dripping cave) which are the bane of insomniacs. One wonders, indeed, if Hardy subconsciously heard "stillicide" as "still-icide," as a word suggesting (by analogy with homicide, patricide, and so forth) "the murder of stillness," or "murderous stillness."

The voices are Hardy's "friends," at least now that they are "beyond," and he needs them, but what they assert is their absolute independence of him and of the whole race of survivors:

*Far.* —"Ye mid zell my favourite heifer, ye mid let the
                                        charlock grow,
    Foul the grinterns, give up thrift."
*Far. Wife*—"If ye break my best blue china, children, I
                                        shan't care or ho."

*All*—"We've no wish to hear the tidings, how the people's
                                        fortune's shift;
        What your daily doings are;
    Who are wedded, born, divided; if your lives beat
                                        slow or swift.

    "Curious not the least are we if our intents you make or mar,
        If you quire to our old tune,
    If the city stage still passes, if the weirs still roar afar."

—Thus, with very gods' composure, freed those crosses
                                        late and soon...
                                                            [CP53]

In this we see an aspect of the godliness of the dead, of the Quiet, and a reason for Hardy's worship of them. Like Swinburne's sleepers, they are invulnerable. Love, pain, fate cannot touch them, and their reduced interest in life is the goal toward which Hardy's incipient and defensive pessemism tended—"Pessimism ... is ... playing the sure ·game.... You cannot lose; you may gain" (L311). The dead cannot lose. They cannot be disappointed or disillusioned. They are not subject to self-division, to the round of loss and return. The Hardy who was fond of dying before he was out of the flesh, and who found the passing of life unbearable, embraces the dead, who, like the ghost he sought to make of himself, have presence but no present. Just as he viewed himself as not solid enough to influence his environment, so the dead in their indifference, in their renunciation of power, become invincible. For Hardy, man possesses only what he has lost, and he loses all that he possesses. The dead have lost everything—and have gained everything in return:

"We have triumphed: this achievement turns the bane to antidote,
  Unsuccesses to success,
Many thought-worn eves and morrows to a morrow free of thought.

"No more need we corn and clothing, feel of old terrestrial stress;
  Chill detraction stirs no sigh;
Fear of death has even bygone us: death gave all that we possess."
[CP53]

The dead are the most impossible and inaccessible of Hardy's lovers, fascinating him in proportion to their distance. They refuse to need him, but their refusal only convinces him of the justness of his desire.

This is half of the story, and insofar as it tells of a yearning for the immortality of oblivion, for a stoic and inhuman quiet, it is perhaps the less attractive half. But the dead have achieved their power at the price of a terrible weakness, and Hardy throws himself into the service of their helplessness. If he escapes into the pastness of the present, he also battles to preserve the presence of the past, striving, as always, to cherish and commemorate the downcast, to touch them and bring them back into touch. Consciousness is pain, but pain is life, and though Hardy flees the necessity of loss, he returns to embrace the possibilities of living.

Compared with the majority of Hardy's dead, those of "Friends Beyond" are unusually self-sufficient, which is why they tend to emphasize the poet's detachment at the expense of his commit-

ment. In "The Haunter," both Hardy and the ghost have profound, incommunicable needs which mirror the longing of the
quiet of the cosmos and the silence of man for each other:

> He does not think that I haunt here nightly:
>   How shall I let him know
> That whither his fancy sets him wandering
>   I, too, alertly go?—
> Hover and hover a few feet from him
>   Just as I used to do,
> But cannot answer the words he lifts me—
>   Only listen thereto!
>
> When I could answer he did not say them:
>   When I could let him know
> How I would like to join in his journeys
>   Seldom he wished to go.
> Now that he goes and wants me with him
>   More than he used to do,
> Never he sees my faithful phantom,
>   Though he speaks thereto.
>
> Yes, I companion him to places
>   Only dreamers know,
> Where the shy hares print long paces,
>   Where the night rooks go;
> Into old aisles where the past is all to him,
>   Close as his shade can do,
> Always lacking the power to call to him,
>   Near as I reach thereto!
>
> What a good haunter I am, O tell him!
>   Quickly make him know
> If he but sigh since my loss befell him
>   Straight to his side I go.
> Tell him a faithful one is doing
>   All that love can do
> Still that his path may be worth pursuing,
>   And to bring peace thereto.

[CP324–25]

The ghost is that of Emma, Hardy's first wife. The greatness of the
loss gives to Hardy the words he never had, but when he listens
there is no answer, and the poem is his attempt to imagine it. What

he seizes from the ominous silence is another and equally frustrated listener. Hardy speaks but cannot hear, while the ghost hears but cannot tell him.

With this, we again approach Tennyson's *In Memoriam*:

> For this alone on Death I wreak
> The wrath that garners in my heart:
> He put our lives so far apart
> We cannot hear each other speak.
>
> [LXXXII]

Like Hardy, Tennyson both listens and speaks, and his continued awareness of his loss substantiates his own presence. The cantos of *In Memoriam* in which Tennyson worries that Hallam will forget him are, as Kissane points out, "inversions of a more serious, 'actual' fear that the poet will forget Hallam"—that the past, love, and identity will be denied, that the self will cease to exist.[8] This corresponds to Hardy's fear that the dead may not need us. The Quiet must listen in order that we may speak.

In Hardy, the speaker and the listener correspond to the division of awareness, to the knowing and the unknowing, the present and absent selves. Hardy often wants them to be one, to be simultaneous, but they cannot be, and they go on haunting each other. In one of his finest and most moving poems, he transforms his own outcry into the calling of the inarticulate dead:

> Woman much missed, how you call to me, call to me,
> Saying that now you are not as you were
> When you had changed from the one who was all to me,
> But as at first, when our day was fair.
>
> Can it be you that I hear? Let me view you, then,
> Standing as when I drew near to the town
> Where you would wait for me: yes, as I knew you then,
> Even to the original air-blue gown!
>
> Or is it only the breeze, in its listlessness
> Travelling across the wet mead to me here,
> You being ever dissolved to wan wistlessness,
> Heard no more again far or near?
>
> Thus I; faltering forward,
> Leaves around me falling,

Leaves oozing thin through the thorn from norward,
  And the woman calling.

[CP325–26]

Hardy describes the connection between self-division and his sense of the past most graphically, if not most artistically, in a fable entitled "He Follows Himself":

> In a heavy time I dogged myself
>   Along a louring way,
> Till my leading self to my following self
>   Said: "Why do you hang on me
>     So harassingly?"
>
> "I have watched you, Heart of mine," I cried,
>   "So often going astray
> And leaving me, that I have pursued,
>   Feeling such truancy
>     Ought not to be."
>
> He said no more, and I dogged him on
>   From noon to the dun of day
> By prowling paths, until anew
>   He begged: "Please turn and flee!—
>     What do you see?"
>
> "Methinks I see a man," said I,
>   "Dimming his hours to gray.
> I will not leave him while I know
>   Part of myself is he
>     Who dreams such dree!"
>
> "I go to my old friend's house," he urged,
>   "So do not watch me, pray!"
> "Well, I will leave you in peace," said I,
>   "Though of this poignancy
>     You should fight free:
>
> "Your friend, O other me, is dead;
>   You know not what you say."
> —"That do I! And at his green-grassed door
>   By night's bright galaxy
>     I bend a knee."

—The yew-plumes moved like mocker's beards
  Though only boughs were they,
And I seemed to go; yet still was there,
  And am, and there haunt we
    Thus bootlessly.

[CP610–11]

This poem, reminiscent of Rossetti's sonnet "He and I," illustrates the necessary opposition of knowing and unknowing, present and past, in Hardy's believing and unbelieving. It "portrays the conflicts within Hardy between the side of his nature that felt, dreamed, and perhaps longed for death, and the side that saw through illusion, distrusted feeling, and labored onward."[9] Knowledge and reason are invulnerable in that they do not have to care what is gone, but they cannot unknow the pastness of the past or, therefore, the certainty of their own end. Feeling and belief are vulnerable, but they preserve what is gone and thus intimate their immortality.

In *The Triumph of Time,* Jerome Buckley chides critics and biographers who too easily identify the passion of the past with infantile escapism and notes that in many cases it is "simply the adult's effort to make his peace with the past and so to come to terms with his present self." Memory is not only an escape from, but also a confrontation of, life, an attempt to "give the brief peremptory moment some semblance of perspective. The meaning of the past remembered lay in its power to enhance the quality of life in the all-demanding present.[10]

It is not always easy to make peace with the past. In the poems we have considered so far, even where loss is crushing, the past is not a threat, and it lives with Hardy in quiet, comfortable domesticity:

We two kept house, the Past and I,
  The Past and I;
Through all my tasks it hovered nigh
  Leaving me never alone.
It was a spectral housekeeping
  Where fell no jarring tone,
As strange, as still a housekeeping
  As ever has been known.

As daily I went up the stair
  And down the stair,
I did not mind the Bygone there—
  The Present once to me;
Its moving meek companionship
  I wished might ever be,
There was in that companionship
  Something of ecstasy.

[CP290]

This is Hardy's normal, homely accommodation with memory. There are, however, other possibilities for the past, such as the ones implied by the poem "Tolerance," and though they are conspicuous in Hardy primarily by their absence, they are nevertheless important:

But now the only happiness
In looking back that I possess—
Whose lack would leave me comfortless—

Is to remember I refrained
From masteries I might have gained,
And for my tolerance was disdained;

For see, a tomb. And if it were
I had bent and broke, I should not dare
To linger in the shadows there.

[CP313]

That is, the past may return not as an obliging household ghost but as an avenging fury. This is the burden of "Wessex Heights":

In the towns I am tracked by phantoms having weird
                              detective ways—
Shadows of beings who fellowed with myself of earlier days:
They hang about at places, and they say harsh heavy things—
Men with a wintry sneer, and women with tart disparagings.

Down there I seem to be false to myself, my simple self that was,
And is not now, and I see him watching, wondering what
                              crass cause
Can have merged him into such a strange continuator as this,
Who yet has something in common with himself, my chrysalis.

I cannot go to the great grey plain; there's a figure
                              against the moon,

Nobody sees it but I, and it makes my breast beat out of tune;
I cannot go to the tall-spired town, being barred by
                    the forms now passed
For everybody but me, in whose long vision they stand there fast.

There's a ghost at Yell'ham Bottom chiding loud at
                    the fall of the night,
There's a ghost in Froom-side Vale, thin-lipped and
                    vague, in a shroud of white,
There is one in the railway train whenever I do not want it near,
I see its profile against the pane, saying what I would not hear.

                              [CP300-301]

Hardy's relentless resurrection of possibilities is potentially dangerous, for ghosts can howl as well as murmur, and it is difficult for him
to find, in a world which he has transformed into a familiar room,
a place where he can be free of memory. It is interesting that when,
as in this poem, Hardy's past becomes unbearable, it is because it
has become too much like the present. It is overpopulated, noisy,
and bustling. It comes with demands and asks for reparations and
decisions. Indeed, the past and the present grow so alike that it is
difficult to determine whether the phantoms of the town in the first
stanza of this excerpt are the living or the dead.

Hardy shares much of Tennyson's sense of the past and present,
especially when, as in "Wessex Heights," he is uneasy. The
achievement of faith in *In Memoriam* parallels the exorcism of the
sense of the watching dead and the guilty, morbid self-consciousness
which inhabit the beginning of the poem:

> Dark house, by which once more I stand
>   Here in the long unlovely street,
>   Doors, where my heart was used to beat
> So quickly, waiting for a hand,
>
> A hand that can be clasp'd no more—
>   Behold me, for I cannot sleep,
>   And like a guilty thing I creep
> At earliest morning to the door.
>
> He *is* not here; but far away
>   The noise of life begins again,
>   And ghastly thro' the drizzling rain
> On the bald street breaks the blank day.

                              [VII]

"Guilty thing" points not only to Tennyson's inadequacy in relation to the overbearing dead, but also, in its allusion to Horatio's description of the apparition of Hamlet's father,[11] to his Hardyan ghostliness in a present which is, like that of Hardy's poem, noisy, urban, crowded, "unlovely," and yet, somehow, even if only in the etymology of "ghastly," ghostly—distant and incomprehensible. Words such as "bald," "noise," "drizzling," "blank" are, for Tennyson as for Hardy, distress signals. They are a diction of mechanism, of monotony, of the incomprehensible and unbearable present whose image is the city. They, along with the emotionally unfulfilling assonantal tightness of the away-again-rain-day endings, lament the homelessness of the spirit, the pounding monotonous demands of a bleak present and a guilty past.

"In Front of the Landscape," the other prominent example of unfriendly haunting in Hardy, also turns on the chaotic and painfully intense presence of the past:

> What were the infinite spectacles featuring foremost
>   Under my sight,
> Hindering me to discern my paced advancement
>   Lengthening to miles;
> What were the re-creations killing the daytime
>   As by the night?
>
> O they were speechful faces gazing insistent,
>   Some as with smiles,
> Some as with slow-born tears that brinily trundled
>   Over the wrecked
> Cheeks that were fair in their flush-time, ash now with anguish,
>   Harrowed by wiles.
>
>                                         [CP285]

Here visions again crowd Hardy with the same insistence as the present, and they come to avenge themselves and to make demands:

> For, their lost revisiting manifestations
>   In their live time
> Much had I slighted, caring not for their purport,
>   Seeing behind

Things more coveted, reckoned the better worth calling
  Sweet, sad, sublime.

Thus do they now show hourly before the intenser
  Stare of the mind
As they were ghosts avenging their slights by my bypast
  Body-borne eyes,
Show, too, with fuller translation than rested upon them
  As living kind.

[CP286–87]

As if in response to the pressures of the situation, Hardy's syntax contorts uncharacteristically. The dead return to complain of his neglect of them while they were alive, and this neglect seems to have resulted from Hardy's fascination with the pluperfect, with what even then was past. "In Front of the Landscape" points to a vicious circle of neglect of the present and guilt in the face of the angry past which could easily have taken control of Hardy. It never did, for Hardy was Hardy, and that was not his way.

Considering the number of poems either obviously or peripherally haunted, we must inevitably conclude that poems like "Wessex Heights" and "In Front of the Landscape" are in a very small minority indeed, for in general, Hardy does not feel, or does not accept, the right of the past to be disappointed in him:

Well, well! All's past amend,
Unchangeable. It must go.
[CP319]

He is beset by omens and haunted relentlessly, and it is remarkable that these visitations should be so empty of any suggestion of guilt. Hardy, for all his obsessions, is a healing poet. He forgets heroically and loses cleanly. He is, as Irving Howe admirably puts it, "free of that version of pride which consists in relentless self-accusation."[12] Hardy is singularly secure about his past, and therefore about himself, and his dead do not, unlike Tennyson's in *In Memoriam*, assume gigantic proportions. Regret is no stranger to him, but his regret is not for what he has done or left undone but for the passing of what was good and beautiful. His only sadness is that life, though it must be loved as all we have, is, after all, too small for us. In saying

131

these things, we excuse his faults, for we have found in him a great and difficult sanity, and we can only step aside to let him prepare his own end.

Hardy was obsessed with lastness, and one of the reasons for his lack of particularization as compared to, say, Browning, is that he tends to define things in terms of their disappearance, in terms of their ending. They touch him in their vanishing. Individuality is as much a matter of death as of life, and when loss struck deeply, he would retrace his path to find "The Last Time":

> The kiss had been given and taken,
>   And gathered to many past:
> It never could reawaken;
>   But I heard none say: "It's the last!"
>
> The clock showed the hour and the minute
>   But I did not turn and look:
> I read no finis in it,
>   As at closing of a book.
>
> But I read it all too rightly
>   When, at a time anon,
> A figure lay stretched out whitely,
>   And I stood looking thereon.
>                               [CP650]

Hardy said, "No man's poetry can be truly judged till its last line is written. What is the last line? The death of the poet" (L302), and in poetry, as in life, he died more than once before his time. Though he did not write a "Crossing the Bar," he refused to let the final blow catch him unprepared, and each of his last four volumes ends with a poem or group of poems which amount to a farewell to life and to art. He put his death behind him in order to possess it, and his final wish was to have the last word. It is the one wish that the living can grant:

> HE RESOLVES TO SAY NO MORE
>   O my soul, keep the rest unknown!
>   It is too like the sound of moan
>     When the charnel-eyed
>     Pale Horse has nighed:
>   Yea, none shall gather what I hide!

Why load men's minds with more to bear
That bear already ails to spare?
  From now alway
  Till my last day
What I discern I will not say.

Let Time roll backward if it will;
(Magians who drive the midnight quill
  With brain aglow
  Can see it so,)
What I have learnt no man shall know.

And if my vision range beyond
 The blinkered sight of souls in bond,
  —By truth made free—
  I'll let all be,
 And show to no man what I see.

[CP887]

# NOTES

NOTES TO CHAPTER ONE

1. Donald Davie, *Thomas Hardy and British Poetry* (London: Routledge & Kegan Paul, 1973), p. 11.

2. CP92 equals Thomas Hardy, *The Collected Poems of Thomas Hardy*, 4th ed. (London: Macmillan, 1930 [1962 printing]), p. 92. The *Collected Poems* commonly sold by Macmillan in the U. S. is a reprint of the 1925 edition. It lacks *Winter Words*, it has no alphabetical index of titles, and its pagination is slightly different from that of the fourth edition.

3. Thomas Hardy, *Two on a Tower* (New York: Harper & Bros., 1905), p. 8.

4. Harold Bloom, *The Ringers in the Tower* (Chicago: University of Chicago Press, 1971), pp. 19-20.

5. L185 equals Florence Emily Hardy, *The Life of Thomas Hardy* (London: Macmillan, 1962), p. 185.

6. Robert Langbaum, *The Poetry of Experience* (New York. Norton, 1963), p. 49.

7. David Perkins, "Hardy and the Poetry of Isolation," in *Hardy: A Collection of Critical Essays*, ed. Albert J. Guerard, *Twentieth Century Views* (Englewood Cliffs, N. J.: Prentice Hall, 1963), pp. 151-52.

8. Ibid., p. 152.

9. J. O. Bailey, *The Poetry of Thomas Hardy: A Handbook and Commentary* (Chapel Hill, N. C.: University of North Carolina Press, 1970), p. 179.

10. J. Hillis Miller, *Distance and Desire* (Cambridge, Mass.: Harvard University Press, 1970), pp. 3, 190.

11. Paul Zietlow, *Moments of Vision* (Cambridge, Mass.: Harvard University Press, 1974), pp. 33-34.

12. Miller, *Distance and Desire*, p. 204.

13. Ibid., p. 210.

14. Ibid., chapter 8, passim.

15. Richard Howard, *Untitled Subjects* (New York: Atheneum, 1969), dedication.

## NOTES TO CHAPTER TWO

1. Samuel Hynes, *The Pattern of Hardy's Poetry* (Chapel Hill, N. C.: University of North Carolina Press, 1961), p. 131.

2. B336 equals Robert Browning, *The Complete Poetical Works of Robert Browning* (Cambridge, Mass.: Houghton Mifflin, 1895), p. 336.

3. J. Hillis Miller, *The Disappearance of God: Five Nineteenth Century Writers* (Cambridge, Mass.: Harvard University Press, 1963), pp. 84-85.

4. Ibid., pp. 95, 97.

5. Bloom, *Ringers*, p. 158.

6. W. David Shaw, *The Dialectical Temper: The Rhetorical Art of Robert Browning* (Ithaca, N. Y.: Cornell University Press), 1968, p. 11.

7. Langbaum, *Poetry of Experience*, pp. 79-80.

8. Donald Davie, *Thomas Hardy and British Poetry* (New York: Oxford University Press, 1972), p. 62.

9. V. H. Collins, *Talks with Thomas Hardy* (Garden City, N. Y.: Doubleday, 1928), p. 7.

10. Jean Brooks, *Thomas Hardy: The Poetic Structure* (Ithaca, N. Y.: Cornell University Press, 1971), p. 107.

11. Hynes, *Pattern of Hardy's Poetry*, pp. 44-45.

12. Thomas Hardy, *The Mayor of Casterbridge* (New York: Harper & Bros., 1905), pp. 213-14.

13. Hynes, *Pattern of Hardy's Poetry*, p. 11.

14. Ibid., p. 62.

## NOTES TO CHAPTER THREE

1. R. G. Cox, ed., *Thomas Hardy: The Critical Heritage* (New York: Barnes & Noble, 1970), p. 319.

2. Ibid., pp. 323, 324.

3. Ibid., p. 325, 327.

4. Davie, *Hardy and British Poetry*, p. 5.

5. Hynes, *Pattern of Hardy's Poetry*, p. 124.

6. "He [Hardy] tried also to avoid being touched by his playmates. One lad, with more insight than the rest, discovered the fact: 'Hardy, how is it that you do not like us to touch you?' This peculiarity never left him, and to the end of his life he disliked even the most friendly hand being laid on his arm or shoulder." (L25)

7. Miller, *Disappearance*, p. 119, 123.

8. Brooks, *Hardy: Poetic Structure*, p. 45.

9. Ibid., p. 46.

10. John Crowe Ransom, ed. *Selected Poems of Thomas Hardy* (New York Macmillan, 1966) Collier Paperback p.xii.

11. Hynes, *Pattern of Hardy's Poetry*, p. 63.

12. Ibid., p. 75.

13. Ibid., p. 74.

14. Harold Orel, ed., *Thomas Hardy's Personal Writings* (Lawrence, Kansas: University Press of Kansas, 1966), pp. 80-81.

15. Davie, *Hardy and British Poetry*, *pp. 18-19, 20*.

16. Ibid., p. 23.

17. C. H. Salter, "Unusual Words Beginning with Un, En, Out, Up and On in Thomas Hardy's Verse, " *Victorian Poetry* 11, no 3:257-61, 257.

NOTES TO CHAPTER FOUR

1. Hynes, *Pattern of Hardy's Poetry*, p. 41.

2. Delmore Schwartz, "Poetry and Belief in Thomas Hardy," in Guerard, ed., *Hardy: Collection of Critical Essays*, pp. 128-129.

3. James Kissane, "Tennyson: The Passion of the Past and the Curse of Time," *ELH* 32 (1965);85-109, p. 100.

4. Bailey, *Poetry of Thomas Hardy: Handbook and Commentary*, pp. 145-47.

5. Thomas Hardy, *The Trumpet-Major* (New York: Harper and Bros., 1905), p. 46.

6. Hynes, *Patterns of Hardy's Poetry*, p. 40.

7. Bailey, *Poetry of Thomas Hardy: Handbook and Commentary*, p. 576.

8. Kissane, *"Tennyson: Passion of the Past,"* p. 100.

9. Bailey, *Poetry of Thomas Hardy: Handbook and Commentary*, p. 472.

10. Jerome Hamilton Buckley, *The Triumph of Time: A Study of Vic-*

*torian Concepts of Time, History, Progress, Decadence* (Cambridge, Mass.: Harvard University Press, 1967), pp. 112-13, 115.

11. Robert W. Hill, Jr., ed., *Tennyson's Poetry* (New York: Norton, 1971), p. 124, n. 4.

12. Irving Howe, *Thomas Hardy* (New York: Macmillan, 1967), p. 185.

# INDEX

139